W9-CBR-914

Inclusion:
A Practical Guide
for
Parents

Tools to Enhance Your Child's Success in Learning

Lorraine O. Moore, Ph.D.

Peytral Publications

Minnetonka, Minnesota

Inclusion: A Practical Guide for Parents - Tools to Enhance Your Child's Success in Learning.

by Lorraine O. Moore

Published by:

Peytral Publications
P.O. Box 1162
Minnetonka, MN 55345
(612) 949-8707   Fax (612) 906-9777

All rights reserved. No part of this book may be used or reproduced in any manner without written permission from the publisher, except for brief quotations embodied in critical articles and reviews.

Copyright ©1996 Peytral Publications. All rights reserved.
First Printing 1996
Printed and bound in the United States of America

Publisher's Cataloging in Publication
(Prepared by Quality Books, Inc.)

Moore, Lorraine O.
    Inclusion: A Practical Guide for Parents - Tools to Enhance Your Child's Success in Learning. / Lorraine O. Moore
        p. cm.
    Includes bibliographical references.
    ISBN 0-9644271-3-3

    1. Handicapped children--Education. 2. Mainstreaming in education.
3. Special Education -- Planning. -- 4. Parenting--Study and training. I. Title.
II. Title: Tools to Enhance your Child's Sucess in Learning

LC4015.M66 1996   371.9'046
                          QBI96-20257

Library of Congress Catalog Card Number   96-067057

TABLE OF CONTENTS

PREFACE

This book was written to acknowledge all parents who support and nourish the learning efforts of their children. It was especially written for parents who have children identified as having a disability, which increases the challenge of learning for the child and adds additional responsibilities to parents.

The ideas presented in this book have come from being a parent of two children and the years of personal experience in both public and private schools as a teacher, counselor, and psychologist. The multitudinous contributions of the outstanding educators, dedicated parents, and insightful children of the Eden Prairie School District in Minnesota are responsible for the evolution of the thoughts and ideas represented in this book. I especially want to thank and acknowledge Peggy Hammeken, who encouraged me to write this book, and without whose support, it probably would not have happened.

The expertise and support of my editor, Jennet Grover, greatly assisted the writing and molding of this book into its present form.

I dedicate this book to my two children, Jane and John, who, from an early age, have given me invaluable insights about children and parenting.

INTRODUCTION

Inclusive schooling, the practice of educating children with and without disabilities together rather than separately, is emerging in schools throughout the United States. As more and more schools are adopting inclusion, parents and educators are being met with new challenges to meet the needs of students experiencing difficulties in learning due to various handicapping conditions. Children who have difficulty processing information and/or difficulty maintaining a reasonable attention span call for an educational atmosphere integrating a creative approach and a strong commitment to addressing their learning requirements. This book is written for the purpose of helping parents face these challenges and providing new ways of assisting their children in the learning process.

Inclusion has provided the scenario that now allows and encourages parents, educators, and school staff to work together to better ensure success for children with disabilities.

Background information has been provided for parents about the way children learn. The specific difficulties children with learning disabilities and attention deficits encounter in the learning process are addressed, in addition to ways parents can learn more about how their particular child learns.

Several strategies have been provided for parents to use to help their children benefit to a greater degree from all learning experiences. These strategies can be applied to create better learning environments for children at home and at school by addressing specific ways to help children with their reading, math, and writing skills.

Ways are presented for parents to measure their individual child's learning progress, including both formal ways (standardized tests) and informal ways (teacher observation, assessment of daily work, etc.).

Sample forms are included for parents to use with their child, and in communicating with educators. These may be reproduced for your use as needed.

A listing of some specific reference books has been provided that can enlarge your resource library and expand your awareness of learning styles, learning strategies, and other topics that are of interest to parents of children with disabilities. Also included is a listing of organizations that parents can contact for additional information about their child's disability. Some of these organizations may be a useful resource for parent advocacy.

After considerable thought, a decision was made to use the pronoun "he," as it complies with standard literary practice, instead of using both "he" and "she," which became extremely cumbersome for the reader. Unfortunately, until the literary community comes up with some reasonable facsimile that makes a less gendered alternative, we find ourselves forced to take the more traditional approach for the sake of clarity and simplicity.

This book has been written with a great deal of love for children and a deep respect for the role parents and educators play in a child's life. It is written as a resource for parents, to act as a catalyst for better understanding their child's learning and ways to support this learning. It is in being successful as a learner that contributes to a child's positive feelings about himself. It is the responsibility of the parents and other adults in a child's life to encourage and support this success in learning. Herein lies our future.

CHAPTER ONE

INCLUSIVE EDUCATION - A SHARED RESPONSIBILITY

All children can learn. The question is "Under what conditions can each child learn best?" In the case of a child with a disability, can he learn best in the regular classroom setting with his peers or in a resource room setting with other children who have disabilities? The practice of **inclusion** supports the regular classroom setting as providing the best learning environment for most children with a disability.

This chapter explores what inclusion is, and its benefits for children who have difficulty learning as a result of one or more disabilities.

WHAT IS INCLUSION?

Inclusion means teaching children with disabilities in regular education classrooms right beside children without disabilities. Inclusion means the special education teacher goes to the child, rather than the child going to the special education teacher.

The idea of inclusion dates back to the passage of the Education for All Handicapped Children Act of 1975. This law states that all students have a right to be educated in the least restrictive environment. Due to the term *least restrictive* being interpreted as *separate*, we have been experiencing a dual system of education - one for children with disabilities and one for children without disabilities.

After the passage of this law, children with disabilities attended regular classes part of the time, but received all of their basic skills instruction in a *Resource Room*. They continued to get their basic skills instruction in reading, math, written language, speech, language development, etc. in this setting until their skill level was developed to a point where they could be integrated back into the regular classroom for those subjects (see Figure 1). For some children, this meant being out of their regular classroom for 1 or 2 hours; for children with more severe disabilities, it meant being out of the classroom the greater part of the school day.

In the early 1980's and especially from 1986 on, there has been a concentrated effort on the part of school districts to redefine its placement practices. *Least restrictive environment,* as currently defined, means educating children with disabilities in the same classrooms as children without disabilities to the greatest extent possible. This movement to change the meaning of *inclusion* has been bolstered by recent research showing not only positive results in children's learning, but more importantly, in their *attitude* towards learning when they receive their special education services in the regular classroom.

The passage of the Individuals with Disabilities Act and Americans with Disabilities Act have further created a basis for a national policy that focuses on the inclusion, independence and empowerment of individuals with disabilities. Court decisions have continually upheld the right of each child to be educated in a public school in a regular classroom setting. As a result of these actions, there has been a new interpretation given to the concept of inclusion by some school districts. The model for educating children with disabilities now looks like this:

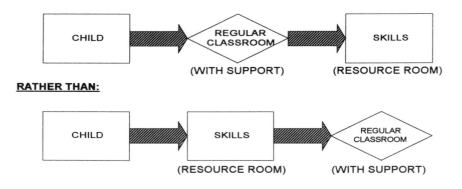

FIGURE 1

In the new model, your child receives all his services in the regular classroom setting. If your child does not make satisfactory progress, with the support and modifications made in the classroom setting, consideration is given to have some of your child's needs met in the resource setting. A decision regarding this option comes only after you and your child's educational team meet to decide if this change is in the best interests of your child. Under the old model, your child would have started receiving his special education services in the resource room.

The meaning of inclusion, as shown by the previous two models, are the two most common interpretations given to inclusion by school districts. The trend toward moving into the new model is becoming more predominant in schools across the United States. Important to note is that this model is based on a continuum of special education services. This is in contrast to some school districts which have chosen to move toward a *full inclusion* model. In a full inclusion model, all children with disabilities receive their special education services within the regular classroom setting only.

THE NEW MODEL OF INCLUSION

What does inclusion look like based on the new model in Figure 1? First, special education teachers come into your child's regular classroom setting. Second, your child's special education teacher and regular education teacher set up a team approach to teaching your child in the classroom setting. Together, they plan lessons and deliver instructions that will meet your child's academic and social/emotional needs. They also share responsibility for assessing your child's learning progress and mastery of subject matter. Here are some possible ways for this to happen:

♦ One teacher teaches the large group while the other teacher circulates around the room, paying particular attention to the needs of the children with disabilities.

♦ The teachers divide the class into two parts, each teaching the same information to a select group.

♦ One of the teachers provides remediation (re-teaching) for children who need it (those with disabilities and those without), while the other provides enrichments (further expansion of the subject matter) for the rest of the class.

♦ Both teachers teach the whole group at the same time, one modeling or demonstrating a skill while the other describes it.

In some schools, children with disabilities are clustered together in one or more classes at each grade level for subjects like reading, written language and math. A special education teacher then comes into each of these classes every day to team teach with the classroom teacher.

If your child is placed in an inclusion setting for the first time, you will find it helpful to use Forms 1 and 2 in Appendix A to review each of your reactions to a regular classroom environment. This feedback can then be shared with your child's teachers or educational team.

THE BENEFITS OF INCLUSION

Inclusion carried out in one or more of these ways increases the communication between regular education teachers and special education teachers. Through this communication, special education teachers develop a better understanding of classroom curriculum and regular education teachers develop a better understanding of the needs of children with disabilities. Both groups of teachers develop better ways to modify curriculum, and develop reasonable expectations across all subjects where needed for your particular child. They can also, working together, develop more efficient and effective strategies for your child to use in acquiring skills. The combined expertise and resources of general education and special education programs and services maximize the learning benefits for your child.

Inclusion allows your child to exercise a basic right, the right to be educated with his peers. It emphasizes an unconditional acceptance of your child as a child, without undue focus put on his disabilities. Your child's school life becomes a holistic approach to learning by participating in all facets of school life rather than being fragmented into discrete parts based on needs that arise from his limitations. With the practice of inclusion, your child can feel like a *regular kid* and still get the special help he needs.

The need to feel that one belongs is a basic human need, according to Abraham Maslow's theory of psychology. Maslow pointed out that belonging was an essential and prerequisite human need that had to be met before one could achieve a sense of self-worth. For some children, a degree of this sense of self-worth can come from achievement. For children who have difficulty learning, it becomes critical that this sense of belonging provides the basis for self-worth. In turn, a positive self-worth provides the motivation for a child to put more effort into his learning. Belonging also has a social context and implications for the child's future performance in society.

WHAT IS NEEDED FOR INCLUSIVE SCHOOLING

As more and more schools are adopting the practice of inclusive schooling, parents and educators are being met with new challenges. To meet these challenges, more creative approaches and collaborative efforts are necessary to meet the learning, and social and emotional needs of children with disabilities. Inclusion provides individualized care to children with disabilities, while forcing the teaching system to expand and be creative in order to meet the growing needs of the times.

❧

CHAPTER TWO
❧❧❧

COLLABORATION: WORKING TOGETHER

Inclusion is most successful for children when it is based on collaborative efforts between parents and school. It is a team effort that should involve working together effectively and providing mutual support. A collaborative model for sharing ideas and making decisions is the foundation of inclusion.

Meeting the learning needs of children with disabilities in a regular educational setting challenges our creativity for adapting curriculum, developing appropriate teaching strategies, and structuring the learning environment. Success in meeting this challenge requires the joint cooperation of parents and educators on a continual basis through a team effort.

As a parent, keep in mind that you are a valuable member of your child's educational team (designated as a multidisciplinary team on your child's Individual Educational Plan). Your input is needed. You know your child best. You not only experience your child's feelings about school and learning on a day-to-day basis, but also know what learning has been like for your child on a year-to-year basis.

You know and understand your child's strengths and limitations. When your child feels good about learning, you feel good about your child's education. When things do not go well for your child, you want to find out why and want to know what changes need to be made to remedy the situation. As a member of your child's team, you can communicate this information to the team members who are responsible for your child's progress in learning.

Educators bring their expertise about learning to the team. How your child is progressing in his particular learning is important information educators can provide. They also are an excellent resource on how children learn and how to create the best learning environment for your child at school.

Together, educators and parents can share ideas and make decisions as to the best ways to meet your child's needs. It then becomes the *school's* responsibility to teach and monitor your child's success in acquiring knowledge and skills. It becomes *your* responsibility to support your child and the school in this process. It is also important that *you* follow through with your child on his homework assignments and special projects.

When your child has a disability that interferes with his ability to acquire and maintain satisfactory progress, it takes more time, commitment, and involvement on your part to keep an open communication with the school. It continuously involves being in touch with your child's teachers, while also being in touch with your child's feelings, and knowing how to best support the efforts of your child and the school. Ways to be in touch with your child's feelings will be discussed in Chapter 4. Supporting the efforts of your child will be addressed in Chapters 6 and 7. The remainder of this chapter will be devoted to parents' involvement with the school community.

THE SCHOOL COMMUNITY

Working collaboratively with the school community is dependent upon the sharing of information between parents and educators. There are three basic aspects to this sharing. One involves the information you can share about your child with your child's teachers. A second type of sharing is the information you can gain about your child from school staff. The third aspect of this sharing involves ways in which this information can be exchanged between parents and educators. Each of these three aspects will be discussed in the following paragraphs.

PARENT'S KNOWLEDGE OF THEIR CHILD

Parents should attempt to share with educators relevant information regarding their child's:

- disability

- strengths and limitations, both as a person and as a learner

- interests and hobbies

- fears and concerns about learning and about school

- most favorite and least favorite school subjects

- health concerns

- feelings about self as a person and as a learner

- needs

- learning patterns and styles, if noticeable

- family traumas, transitions, etc.

[See Form 3 in Appendix A for ways to record this information.]

SCHOOL'S KNOWLEDGE OF YOUR CHILD

Information you can get from educators about your child include:

- how your child is performing in all areas of school, including learning content and work habits

- the results of any standardized testing that was completed on your child in the areas of achievement, intellectual ability, language development, motor development, etc.

- the results of informal testing on your child such as teacher-made tests and work samples in all subject areas documentation of your child's areas of strengths as a person and as a learner

- identification and documentation of the problem areas your child is experiencing

- documentation about the degree of severity regarding your child's disability (from mild to severe)

- documentation of the reasons your child is having difficulty learning in one or more subjects (i.e., processing difficulties)

- if and what curriculum adaptations are being used to accommodate your child's disability

- the instructional strategies being used to help your child be successful in an inclusion setting

- what modifications in assignments are being made for your child, such as decreasing the amount of assignments, modification of written work requirements, tests, etc.

[You may wish to have these last three items documented on Form 4, found in Appendix A.]

- the school's expectations for learning progress relative to your child's areas of disability

- grading practices and any modifications in grading being used to chart your child's progress

- observations regarding your child's learning patterns and learning style

- observations regarding your child's social and emotional development

- what you can do to support your child's learning needs at home

- other questions and information you need relative to your child's disability and educational needs

NOTE: This information is documented on your child's Individual Educational Plan and reviewed periodically.

HOME/SCHOOL COMMUNICATION

There are several different ways for parents to communicate with the school community and be an active part of that community. Some of these are standard ways the school has set up for providing communication between parents and the school. Other ways are prescribed by Federal and State Guidelines for parents who have a child with a disability.

Other options include ways that you can initiate contact with school staff as needed. Some of the forms of communication are a one-way process meant as a matter of information for you. Other forms of communication require your acknowledgment of the information and/or more extensive interaction with school staff. The primary people you will be interacting with are your child's regular education teachers and your child's special education teachers.

Other school staff available to you include the principal, school psychologist, school social worker, school counselor, school nurse, and any other support personnel within your school district.

Two of the most common ways for schools to communicate a child's progress to parents are through the report card and through parent/teacher conferences. Report cards are issued up to four times a year, whereas parent conferences take place twice a year. Together, these two forms of communication give you a general sense of your child's progress.

For parents whose child has been identified as having a disability, a multi-disciplinary team (made up of your child's teachers and other key school staff involved with your child's learning) provides a format for ongoing communications. Initially, you are involved with this team when assessment results from testing your child are shared with you and a decision is made as to your child's program placement and how your child's educational needs can be met. This team format can provide you with much of the information mentioned previously.

Any questions you have about your child's disability and specific learning needs can be addressed at the initial meeting or at any other future meeting. This is also an opportunity for you to bring the information you feel is important for school staff to know about your child. The information shared and decisions made about your child at this team meeting will be summarized and documented in your child's Individual Educational Plan. The team can be reconvened at your request or any of your child's teachers' request at any time to review the progress of your child and evaluate the effectiveness of the learning interventions being done.

This team is required to meet at least once a year (called a periodic review) in the event no one makes a request to meet sooner. A parent on his child's multidisciplinary team is considered a valuable member and has the same rights and responsibilities for educational decisions about his child as any other team member. As noted earlier, a collaborative process between you and school staff is the most effective method of bringing about positive results for your child.

A collaborative approach is especially important in cases where differing opinions occur between you and school staff or among the school staff itself. The collaborative process provides a means by which differences can be resolved by everyone contributing their ideas. These ideas are then combined into workable solutions that are in the best interest of your child.

It is important for you to be involved with your child's educational team when there is:

♦ a need for significant change to be made in your child's current placement or program.

♦ a need to add or delete a special education service.

♦ a change in the setting in which your child receives special education services.

♦ a modification needed in his IEP (Individual Education Plan).

♦ a need to increase or decrease the amount of special education services provided in order to meet your child's individual goals.

Sometimes a physician or agency outside the school community will make a recommendation regarding placement and program for your child. When this occurs, you should take this recommendation to your child's primary or homeroom teacher. In most cases, the teacher would then take this recommendation to your child's educational or multidisciplinary team. The team would then meet (with you present) to review the recommendation and determine the appropriateness of the recommendation relative to the school's data about your child.

If you find that your interactions with the communication systems of the school and your child's educational team are not sufficient for keeping current on your child's progress, you may initiate additional communication with school community members. This communication is generally initiated and planned with your child's regular education teachers in conjunction with your child's special education teachers.

Communications available to you generally involve a daily or weekly written report by a designated teacher. This can be in the form of a notebook or weekly folder. Your child should be given the responsibility to give this to you and return it back to the designated teacher when this is appropriate. He should also know why this is being done and how it can help him.

Your child's level of involvement in his educational program is dependent upon age. Younger children can be involved at the level of participating in parent/teacher conferences, carrying communications between school and home, sharing his feelings about school and about himself as a learner. Older children can and should be involved at all levels possible, including being present at their educational team meetings.

Collaboration works best when there is joint ownership and responsibility. Regular education and special education teachers share responsibility for your child's education. Parents share responsibility as an advocate for ensuring their child's success through communicating with educators and their child. Children are involved in the planning of their education, as appropriate, and in sharing their successes and concerns with parents and educators. The total process is one of taking responsibility jointly for the input and outcome of the child's education.

The remainder of this book will be devoted to information that is organized to provide parents with a greater degree of understanding of their child as a learner, how to chart their child's progress, and how to support their child in the learning process. As you read these pages, remember how much you already know about your child and the support you are already giving your child.

CHAPTER THREE

WHY SOME CHILDREN HAVE DIFFICULTY LEARNING

This chapter is concerned primarily with two different groups of children who *want* to learn, but find learning school subjects difficult and very frustrating. The first group includes those children who have been tested and found to have a **Learning Disability** in reading, math, and/or written language. The second group of children consists of children who have been diagnosed as having an **Attention Deficit Disorder**. Together, both groups of children make up about 8% - 12% of our school population.

When talking about these children, it is extremely important that we remember first and foremost that they are human beings and secondly, that they have been diagnosed as having a learning difficulty and/or attention problem. We do not want to lose sight of the whole child when responding to his area of difficulty.

INFORMATION PROCESSING

The academic subjects of reading, math and writing will be our main focus for elaborating on skills and abilities involved in the learning process. Learning to read or reading to learn, doing math and putting thoughts into written form are dependent upon a student's ability to pay attention and process information using several different skills or abilities.

Grouped together, these subject areas require the child to focus and pay attention to what is being presented, organize the information, process it, and then put the data into long term memory, verbalize it, or reproduce it in writing. The following is a model to illustrate this process.

THE INFORMATION PROCESSING SYSTEM FOR LEARNING

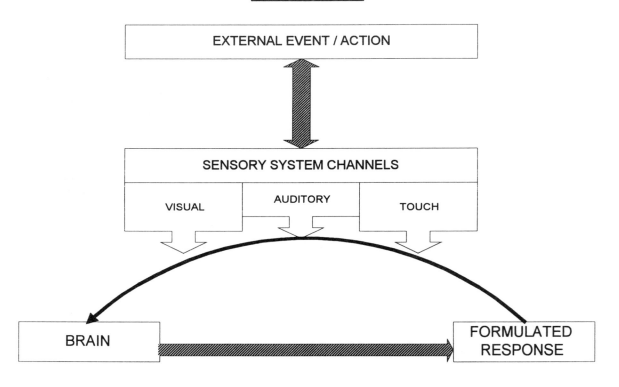

FIGURE 2

As noted in this model, an external event, such as a book or a teacher, activates one or more of the sensory system channels. This information is then transmitted to the brain. The brain receives, organizes, and acts on the information, using one or more of the psychological processes needed to mentally manipulate and make sense of the information received. After a period of time ranging from immediate to several seconds, the brain formulates a response.

This response is fed back to the sensory system channels, at which time the learner expresses the response either verbally or non-verbally.

For the average learner, the flow of information from one level to the other happens without interruption. For the child with a learning disability and/or attention disorder, the flow is interrupted or broken at one or more points. These breaks in the learning process make it difficult for the child to acquire and process information at the same rate as his peers. Similarly, the lack of focus and the impulsiveness of children with attention problems break the flow of the learning process, thus contributing to their lack of success.

To further add to the complexity of the learning process, each level of information processing requires several skills on the part of the learner to achieve success. As many of these skills cannot be observed directly, we need to make inferences from a child's behaviors while working on specific tasks. We can also objectively record a child's responses to specific test items designed to measure processing skills. For parents whose child has been identified through testing as having a learning disability, there should be documentation on the child's assessment that helps identify what areas of processing difficulties exist.

To better understand a child who has a learning disability, it is good to keep in mind that learning involves all of the senses interacting with information and experiences. For purposes of understanding the child with a learning disability, it is the processing of information that will attract most of our attention. This is the key point. It is for this reason that children with a diagnosed learning disability have difficulty learning at a rate that is consistent with their measured intelligence. This is the result of having difficulty taking in information, doing something with it internally, and then sharing the information in some way. This, in turn, affects how well they do on a day-to-day basis in school, and consequently, how well they do on tests. For the child who has been diagnosed as having an Attention Deficit Disorder, his difficulties in learning are due to an inability to focus and sustain attention on information being presented.

Younger children who fall into one of these groups generally have the most difficulty learning to read. Some children have difficulty acquiring math skills, and some children have difficulty verbalizing what they have learned or being able to put what they have learned into writing. Older children with a learning disability have difficulty when the learning is dependent upon reading. When older children have an Attention Deficit Disorder, it generally results in incomplete tasks.

The ability to do reading and math is initially affected by the learner's ability to focus, pay attention, and discriminate visually and auditorily. Also, the learner must be able to remember what he is seeing and/or hearing.

MEMORY

Remembering information involves three different types of memory. **Short-term memory** involves taking in information and immediately repeating it back to someone or putting in down on paper. **Intermediate-memory** involves holding information in one's memory bank for at least 30 seconds and then either repeating it back in the same form or using the information to solve a problem. An example would be if the subject were given the situation 5+4, and responded with 9. The third type of memory, **long-term memory**, is mainly needed at the levels of processing and output for mentally manipulating information and retrieving information from one's memory bank. This stored information is often needed for future learning.

OBSERVED BEHAVIORS

The following is a list of some of the most noticeable behaviors that a parent might see if their child is having attention, discrimination, and/or memory problems at the input level. He:

- has difficulty following directions (oral or written)

- does not seem to listen or pay attention

- gets frustrated easily or gives up easily

- has difficulty following a map or diagram

- has difficulty remembering instructions and routine tasks

- has difficulty remembering symbols and words

Once the brain has received information, it must do something with it. It must sort, organize, analyze and/or combine the information in such a way that it is useful for the present or put it into storage for future use. Manipulating and storing information in the brain requires the learner to sustain attention, remember what was received, organize it, combine the information in different ways, and give meaning to the information.

The child who has difficulty with one or more of these internal processes exhibits some of the following behaviors. He:

♦ does not follow through with instructions/information

♦ takes longer to do some tasks than others

♦ often seems to show poor judgment and makes poor decisions

♦ needs concrete examples and demonstrations to understand concepts

♦ needs concrete examples and demonstrations to understand how to perform tasks

♦ has trouble relating previously learned information to similar new situations

♦ has difficulty retaining learned information for an extended period of time

♦ has difficulty memorizing a series of items

♦ has difficulty remembering sequences to problem solving

♦ has difficulty organizing work space

♦ has a poor concept of time

♦ does not plan a project in steps

♦ does not plan a project to be completed by a certain deadline

♦ has difficulty working independently

♦ is easily distracted from a task

SHARING INFORMATION

At the level of sharing information (or output level), a child must translate mental images, words, or symbols into a written form, describe them verbally, or give a response using movement or gestures. Children who have difficulty at this level may feel especially frustrated because they know the response to what was asked, but have problems expressing it. This may be due to difficulties in putting thoughts or ideas into words, visual/spatial difficulties and/or poor motor control for writing. For children with learning disabilities at this level, behaviors observed are that they:

◆ can tell you the answer but have difficulty writing the answer

◆ can respond with, "I know it, but cannot say it."

◆ can give a quick, brief answer or response but not elaborate

◆ are hesitant and show frustration when responding

◆ do not complete the task

◆ write illegibly

◆ take excessive time compared to similarly aged peers

◆ lose their work

[Form 5 in Appendix A provides you with a format to record these three sets of behaviors.]

LEARNING DISABILITY

In attempting to understand and work with the child who has an identified learning disability, it is important for parents and educators to keep a few key points in mind. First, and perhaps the most important point is that these children are not purposely causing their disabilities, and for this reason, patience is of the utmost importance. They would prefer to be considered normal, which is the purpose of this entire process. These children will require a great deal of love and support to get them through their schooling. Second, there are similarities in behaviors among children who have learning disabilities, yet each child has his profile of strengths and limitations. This profile should serve as the framework for understanding and working with that particular child.

Children with learning disabilities also vary from mild to severe in the degree to which their processing difficulties impact their learning. A child with minimal problems at one level of information processing will require less modification of curriculum and expectations for learning compared to a child who has a combination of processing problems. In other words, the more breaks there are in the flow of information processing, the more negative an impact on a child's learning and the more modifications and strategies that will be needed for their success. Breaks in the flow of information processing have the potential to contribute to a child's inability to focus, pay attention, and sustain attention long enough to complete a task.

This situation should be distinguished from the difficulties exhibited by a child who has been diagnosed as having an Attention Deficit Disorder.

ATTENTION DEFICIT DISORDER

Children who are diagnosed as having an Attention Deficit Disorder fall into two types. One of these types includes the child who has an excessive amount of activity along with problems of sustaining attention. This group of children is given the diagnosis of **Attention Deficit Disorder with Hyper-activity (ADHD)**. Children who have attention problems without excessive activity levels are diagnosed as having a generalized **Attention Deficit Disorder (ADD)**. Since most children are diagnosed as ADHD, our discussion will be primarily limited to this group of children.

What is an **Attention Deficit Hyperactivity Disorder**? ADHD is considered to be a neuro-developmental disorder that affects 3% - 5% of school age children. It is classified as a *neuro-disorder*, as it relates to the brain's attending function, and *developmental* to indicate that the symptoms change as a person gets older. ADHD is generally accepted as a hereditary condition that affects more boys than girls (estimated ratios vary from 4:1 to 9:1). ADHD is not a disease; it is the way the brain works. As such, it cannot be cured, but it can be managed.

ADHD needs to be viewed as a multi-faceted condition in that it is considered to be a medical diagnosis, treated through use of medication on some children, but also has behavioral and psychological components which need to be addressed by parents and educators. Most often the behavioral needs of these children are met by designing appropriate programs including self-management techniques. A psychological component is most often addressed through counseling.

The three primary types of behaviors associated with an ADHD diagnosis are inattentiveness, impulsiveness, and hyperactivity. Children who show a significant degree of inattentiveness, but not a significant degree of impulsiveness and hyperactivity are diagnosed as having **Attention Deficit Disorder (ADD)** rather than ADHD. Characteristic of these behaviors is that they are seen in all of the child's environments. They are more pronounced when the child is required to sit still and do academic work, but are also present, usually to a lesser degree, at home, in the neighborhood, etc. This makes it imperative for strong collaborative efforts among the medical community when medication is involved, educators relative to the child's learning progress, and parents relative to coordinating everyone's efforts and managing the child's behaviors at home and in the community.

Behaviors associated with an ADHD diagnosis that are most often seen in the home and neighborhood environments include:

♦ being often "on the go" or often acting as if "driven by a motor"

♦ often fidgeting with hands or feet

♦ often having difficulty playing or engaging in leisure activities alone

♦ often talking excessively

♦ often running about or climbing excessively in situations in which it is inappropriate (in adolescents or adults, this may be limited to subjective feelings of restlessness)

♦ often having difficulty awaiting their turn

♦ often interrupting or intruding on others (e.g., interrupts conversations or games)

♦ often avoiding, disliking or reluctance to engage in tasks that require sustained mental effort (such as homework)

♦ often distracted by what is happening around them

♦ difficulty organizing things and activities

♦ often not completing tasks or chores

♦ often missing details or making careless mistakes while doing something

[See Form 6 in Appendix A for a checklist of these behaviors.]

Children who have a *mild* Attention Deficit Disorder display some of the above behaviors, whereas children who have been diagnosed as having a severe ADHD disorder will display many of the above behaviors. It is these behaviors that interfere with the learning process for these children, as they often miss out on the initial instruction given by the teacher. This means that when it comes time to do the lesson on their own, they either have to guess, or ask someone else how to do it. Once they find out, they need to stay on task (sustain attention) long enough to complete the lesson. This tends to be more of a problem for younger children, but can also cause difficulties for the older child.

Children who are impulsive in addition to being inattentive may act on the instruction before the teacher is finished or not listen to the complete directions. This behavior, in turn, often results in doing the work incorrectly. For a greater understanding of these children, it is important to remember that they are not choosing these behaviors to get us upset or angry at them, but rather as a response to the misfiring of the control system of the brain.

In addition to learning disabilities or Attention Deficit Disorders being reasons why some children have difficulty learning, there are several other disabilities that children can be diagnosed as having that also interfere with learning.

EMOTIONAL/BEHAVIORAL DISORDER

A child with this disorder shows behavioral and emotional responses in school that are significantly different from and inappropriate for those of similarly aged peers. These behaviors or emotional responses, in turn, interfere to a significant extent with the child's learning and/or other children's learning. Children with this disorder often need counseling in addition to specific structures and expectations set up in the school environment.

SPEECH/LANGUAGE IMPAIRMENT

A speech disorder exists when a child has a difficult time correctly reproducing spoken sounds and words, producing words in sequence smoothly and/or producing sounds and words equivalent to other children of similar age. A language disability exists when a child has difficulty expressing needs, ideas, or information. This situation is often accompanied by problems in understanding language as well as the verbal expression of language. These children often get frustrated when they need to express themselves verbally, as they often know more than they can say in words.

MENTAL IMPAIRMENT

Children with this disability have significantly lower intelligence for learning compared to similarly aged peers. Their slower rate of learning and capacity to learn academic subjects impacts the rate at which they acquire skills and the amount of material they can learn in a given time period. They also need to be taught at the concrete or "hands-on" level rather than the abstract level (the level of ideas and concepts).

HEARING IMPAIRMENT

Most hearing impaired children are classified as hard-of-hearing rather than having total loss of hearing. Children who have a hard-of-hearing diagnosis cannot hear the spoken word clearly, but this can often be improved with hearing aids. Educational performance is almost always affected by a hearing impairment. These children need extra visual input compared to the average child their age.

VISUAL IMPAIRMENT

A child who is totally blind must depend on his non-visual senses, primarily hearing and touch, to access information. A child with even a partial visual handicap has an impairment that means, even with correction, the child's educational performance will be compromised. A child with partial sight has a limited ability to see print, even with lenses. All written materials need to be adapted to accommodate these children. Since their senses, other than sight, tend to be more highly developed, these senses should be incorporated into the instructional program to improve their success at learning.

PHYSICAL IMPAIRMENT

A child with this disorder has a physical impairment that adversely affects the child's educational performance. An example of this disability is cerebral palsy. A physical impairment plays out differently for each child in terms of his ability to learn. Individualized programs are needed to accommodate a child's physical impairment.

OTHER HEALTH IMPAIRMENTS

This refers to children who have limited strength or vitality due to chronic or acute health problems such as heart condition, rheumatic fever, asthma, cancer, diabetes, or Acquired Immune Deficiency Syndrome (AIDS). These conditions generally result in absenteeism from school which interferes with the child's learning progress. Often special programs and schedules need to be set up between the home and school so that these children can have continuity in their learning. Televisions that have been hooked up to the child's classroom allow the child to participate in the group learning process, even if he is bedridden.

There are many reasons other than the ones described in this chapter that may contribute to children's lack of success in school. These will not be elaborated on other than to suggest that many of the techniques outlined in the strategy chapters can be used for any child who is having difficulty learning.

CHAPTER FOUR

LEARNING ABOUT YOUR CHILD AS A STUDENT

There are three basic ways for parents to gain information about their child as a learner. They can ask questions of their child directly, they can observe their child in relevant situations, and they can talk to others who work with their child. This chapter will discuss each of these ways and then give ideas for how parents can identify the strengths and learning patterns of their child.

The best starting point and often the best way a parent can learn about his child is to ask the child directly. This can take place using a natural conversation with the child that is based on some key questions and ideas. These questions should be modified and adjusted according to the age of the child. The following can be used by parents to create these conversations.

QUESTIONS ABOUT LEARNING

- ◆ What do you like about reading?
- ◆ What do you find the most difficult for you when reading?

- ◆ What do you enjoy about working with numbers?
- ◆ What parts of math do you find easy? What parts of math do you find difficult?

> ♦ Do you enjoy writing? Why?

Is it easier to tell someone the answer to a question or to write down your answer? What makes it easier? What makes the other way harder?

> ♦ Do you like to write stories? Why?
> ♦ Do you like to write reports? Why?

[See Form 7 in Appendix A for recording your child's answers.]

This type of questioning should help you assess your child's attitude and feelings about learning. Your child's answers to these questions will let you know how your child feels about each of the basic tasks of school learning. It is common to find differences between these areas for most children. This is especially true if your child has been identified as having a learning disability which, in most cases, is in the area of reading and/or written language. Children who have been diagnosed as having an Attention Deficit Disorder often have difficulties across multiple academic subjects.

COMPARING SELF TO OTHERS

It is important for parents to know how their child sees himself as a learner compared to other kids in the same grade level. To gain this information, a parent can ask a question directly or use a graph (Figure 3) as a starting point. If you use the direct verbal approach, appropriate questioning would be: "How do you think you are doing in reading, math, written work, on tests, etc. compared to the other kids in your class?"

For a visual approach, you can use the following graph.

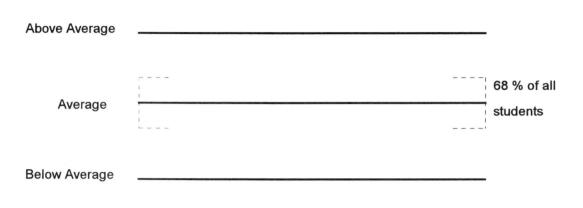

Figure 3

[This graph appears as Form 8 in Appendix A.]

Directions: Have your child put an "x" to show how he is doing in reading, math, written work, and any other school subject compared to other kids at the same grade level. When using this graph with your child, explain that most children and adults fall within the average range (dotted lines) for school subjects. Also explain that some children find it easier to learn and therefore do better at learning than other children, while some other children find it more difficult to learn. It is important to emphasize that all children *can* learn. It is a question of how much and how fast that differs among children.

For a child having difficulty in reading and written work, the completed graph might look like this:

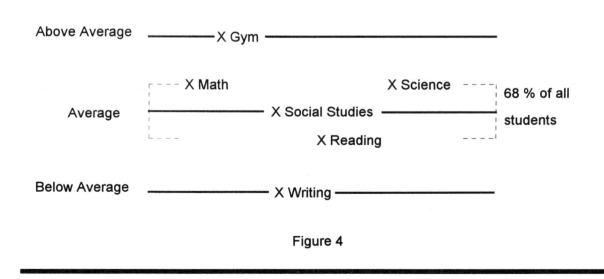

Figure 4

DISCUSSION POINTS

Once a parent finds out how his child sees himself academically in reference to others, the parent can use the following statements and questions as discussion points:

♦ Tell me about your best subjects.

♦ Tell me about the subjects in which you feel you are not doing as well as the other kids.

♦ What changes would you like to make in any of these subjects? What ideas do you have? How can I help you?

♦ Do you have any ideas as to how your teachers can help you?

Questions such as these can give you a better idea of your child's degree of satisfaction with himself as a learner. It can also give you some sense of a child's own resources to change his learning pattern if he is not satisfied with how he is currently doing in one or more subject areas. You can use this information to plan how to help your child in the learning process. It would also be in your child's best interest to share this information with his teachers.

OBSERVATION

The second basic way for parents to gain information about their child as a learner is by observation. Since the "hows" and "whats" to look for vary considerably with the age of a child, this section is divided into two parts. The first part pertains to younger children (up to about age 12), and the second part to older children (13 and up).

Observation is an important way to learn about people as well as about objects and experiences. It is a skill that requires us to really pay attention. In the case of observing people, we not only need to pay attention visually, but also to put aside all judgment and assumptions, to just watch what someone is doing and make note of it. The condition of "no judgments" or "no assumptions" on the part of the observer, in this case the parent, applies to children of all ages. In both cases, it is best to simply jot down what you see and then evaluate what you observe relative to the reason for observing. For our purposes, it is to observe the child's approach to work and completion of a school task.

For younger children, a parent can observe from two perspectives. You can observe your child while he is working independently and you can observe your child's actions when you are working with him. Here are some behaviors to watch for when observing younger children:

♦ Attitude toward doing the task - positive/negative/indifferent?

♦ Organization of materials and work - does he have everything at hand to do the task - Y/N?

♦ Does your child know how to get started -Y/N?

♦ Does your child understand what he needs to do to finish the task - Y/N?

♦ Does your child stay with the task for an appropriate time period - Y/N?

♦ Does your child frequently ask for help - Y/N?

♦ Does the child seem to have the skills necessary to do the task successfully - Y/N?

♦ Does your child take an excessive amount of time to do the task - Y/N?

♦ Does your child give up easily and "shut down" before the task is completed Y/N?

♦ Does your child put down *any* answer just to finish the task - Y/N?

[These questions are also listed as Form 9 in Appendix A to provide you with a format to use while observing and working with your child.]

You may want to observe your child doing different kinds of tasks in various subject areas. It is best to also observe your child more than once doing the same type of task before drawing conclusions. Once you have done this, you can look at your *yes/no* responses to determine the behaviors of your child that help in task completion, and the behaviors that may be interfering with your child's learning. Given this information, you can create a plan with your child to help him change the behaviors that interfere with learning. If it is a matter of not understanding what to do or not seeming to have the skills to do the work, you need to contact your child's teachers and get their support to increase your child's learning success at home.

For older children, observation of their homework habits is a challenge for parents. For this age group, you are limited to what you can observe from a distance and from the objective results of their efforts. For example, you can pay attention to where and under what conditions your child does his work. The "where" is a designated place in the home. The conditions have to do with whether your child works alone or with a classmate and whether the work is done in quiet, with the TV on, with music on, etc.

You can make note of these things until the results of your child's efforts are known via a report card or grade for the particular work done. If either of these is not satisfactory, you then can approach your child as to the possible changes that could be made to improve the results of his efforts.

TALKING TO OTHERS

The third basic way a parent can gain information about his child is to ask other people who work with the child to share how they see the child doing in areas related to school learning.

For all children, regardless of age, a child's teachers are the best source of information. For younger children, daycare workers may also provide some insights for you. When conversing with any of these people, a general question such as, "How is my child doing in _____?" plus some specific questions about work habits and learning progress will give you the most information.

IDENTIFYING STRENGTHS

Unconditional love is the greatest gift parents and educators can give to children. Helping children identify, develop, and nurture their strengths and talents is also necessary. This not only recognizes and supports each child's individuality, but helps the child become who he was meant to be and to feel good about himself.

In helping your child identify his strengths and talents, it is imperative that you approach this process from the child's perspective so as not to impose your wishes and desires upon him. Recognizing and feeling good about one's strengths is especially needed for the child who has difficulty learning in one or more areas of school. There is a tendency for this child to get down on himself because he is not doing well in reading, math, or some other subject. If your child happens to be a perfectionist, he may tend to generalize this feeling to other areas of his life.

Information for identifying your child's strengths can come from a variety of sources. One source is from knowing and understanding the variety of intelligences children (and adults) can have. Currently, the intelligence most understood is the intelligence or ability to learn academic subjects in school. This type of intelligence (referred to as "IQ" by some), is based on one's capacity to learn and solve problems using words, numbers, and spatial patterns. This is the type of intelligence that is related to reading and math, as well as any school subject that is dependent upon these abilities.

This type of intelligence can be divided into verbal abilities and visual/spatial abilities. These abilities can be measured by such well known tests as the Wechsler Intelligence Scale for Children. For some children, their verbal abilities may be more highly developed as compared to their visual/spatial abilities. For other children, it is the reverse. Reading, for example, is more dependent upon a child's language development and verbal abilities than upon his visual/spatial abilities.

If your child has a strength in one or another of these abilities, it will show up in your child's interests and in what school subjects he performs best. Your child's teachers will have a strong sense as to whether your child has more highly developed verbal abilities or more highly developed visual/spatial abilities. For many children, there is no significant difference between the two. In some cases, your child will prefer working with either words or with pictures. If your child appears to have a strength in one or the other, it is important to recognize this strength and help your child recognize it and use it to his advantage.

The work of Howard Gardner has expanded our idea of intelligence to include eight distinct forms of intelligences. Based on these forms, he defines intelligence as *"the capacity to do something useful in society."* Gardner's work not only expands on our view of intelligence, but also puts it into the realm of application, making it useful to the individual and society. This simply means that all children and adults are intelligent when they contribute to society in a useful way.

According to Gardner's work, a person may excel in one or more of the following forms of intelligence: verbal-linguistic, mathematical-logical, spatial, kinesthetic (movement and physical agility), musical, personal, and naturalistic (a special interest in plants and animals). Personal intelligence can be of the type that relates to your child's social relationships (good with people) or of the self-understanding type. Even though, according to Gardner, society favors the mathematical-logical and linguistic (verbal) forms of intelligence, it is imperative that parents and educators recognize all forms of intelligence (the multiple intelligences view) and value them equally.

Parents are the critical link in helping their children identify their strengths from a "multiple intelligences" view rather than from the "traditionalists" view (verbal and visual/spatial abilities only). In this way, parents can nurture their child and encourage the development of his particular abilities. This, in turn, helps in the development of the whole child, not just the development of the "academic child." Paying attention to the development of the whole child is important in the lives of all children, but it is critical in the lives of children who struggle with any part of the learning process.

How your child organizes and processes information is another way to identify your child's strengths. About 50% of our children are equally efficient (or have no preference) in how they organize and process information. Of the remaining 50%, 25% are more efficient when they can process information randomly. The other 25% are more efficient learners when they can process information all at once or in random order. Children with a particular preference can also function the other way, but they will have more success with less effort when they operate through their preferred way.

What does this mean for your child? If your child can organize and process information both *sequentially* and *simultaneously* (randomly) equally well, this is one of your child's strengths. If your child does best with a *sequential* ordering of information, this would be your child's strength. This would mean that your child approaches learning and is more successful when material is presented through a consecutive, step-by-step process. Time, order, and structure are important for this child's success. Since language is dependent upon these concepts, your child may prefer to work with words and verbal or written directions rather than pictures or models.

Children who have a preference for organizing and processing information *simultaneously* need to see the "big picture" before working with the individual parts of an idea or of a specific learning. For example, in math, this child would do better if he saw a model of the completed problem before doing the steps to reach the solution. When given something to put together, this child would tend to work from the picture of the model rather than the directions.

A few characteristics associated with each type of learner appear below.

The Sequential Learner:

♦ likes routine and order in the environment

♦ likes rules and clear expectations

♦ tunes into details

♦ responds well to verbal instruction
   is good at memorizing facts

♦ may be able to read words, but may have trouble comprehending their meaning

♦ likes structure both in time and in how to do things

The Simultaneous Learner:

♦ likes change and flexibility

♦ likes choices

♦ understands the big picture, but may forget facts

♦ responds well to pictures and visual patterns

♦ has difficulty organizing materials and self

♦ is able to draw relationships of past learning to the present learning

♦ finds more value in what he is doing than in fulfilling a time-line or an expectation

[See Form 10 in Appendix A for recording this information.]

If you think your child has a preferential organizing and processing style, observe how your child organizes and responds to the everyday tasks and activities in the home. Observe how your child keeps his room and how he responds to your *verbal* directions versus *showing* him how to do something. This will begin to give you clues about your child's strengths in this area. Also, consult with your child's teachers for additional information.

Identifying a sequential or simultaneous processing strength in your child is especially important for younger children relative to their success in reading. However, it is important for a child of any age to gain a better understanding of how he learns and what learning strategies are best used to ensure his success in learning.

LEARNING STYLES

Identifying a child's learning style is another way we can find out more about a child as a learner. One approach to learning style that has been applied to students and adults is the one developed by Anthony Gregorc. He combined the ideas of abstract and concrete thinking with sequential and random (simultaneous) ordering to create four different learning styles: abstract sequential, concrete sequential, abstract random, and concrete random. These four learning styles are most applicable to children aged 10 through adulthood, but can be used with discretion for younger, school-aged children.

Children and adults who learn and respond to the world from an abstract thinking position tend to do so from the realm of ideas, thoughts, and symbols (non-physical ways). Learning and responding from a concrete level involves experiencing objects and events by a physical or "hands-on" type of approach. We need to be able to do both. However, if a particular child has a preferred way, given a choice, he would tend to interact according to his preferred way.

Gregorc, by combining the ideas of the abstract/concrete and the sequential/random, addresses both the context for learning and ways of responding and ordering our interactions with the world around us. His approach to learning styles gives us a framework from which we can gain more information about a child as a learner.

The following is a brief description of each of Gregorc's four learning styles:

Abstract Sequential (AS):

Abstract Sequential children prefer to interact with the invisible world of ideas and knowledge that are ordered in a logical and structured way. These children rely on thinking to reach conclusions. Their approach to life tends to be serious and realistic. The type of environment in which these children work best is one which is ordered and mentally stimulating.

AS's prefer to function independently rather than have someone work with them or tell them what to do. Children with this dominant style do best in an environment where there are very few distractions. These children are often viewed as being serious and are sometimes referred to as "the little professor."

Concrete Sequential (CS):

For a child or adult who is considered to be of the CS type, it is a "hands-on" approach to experiencing the world. Order and structure are also important to this type of learner. These children are interested in how things work. They like to have things organized and feel good when they have accomplished something. The application of knowledge is more important to these children than the knowledge itself.

A child or adult of this type likes rewards. He performs best in a quiet, ordered, and stable environment where there are clearly explained expectations for behavior and task completion.

Abstract Random (AR):

The "real world" for the dominant AR is the abstract, non-physical world of feelings and emotions (rather than ideas, like the AS). AR children concentrate their energy on relationships. The value of anything, including learning, is based on what has personal meaning for them.

These children do not always pay attention to time, often getting caught up in what they are doing at the moment. They function best in environments that are flexible and allow for freedom of choice and movement rather than those with restrictive rules and regulations.

Concrete Random:

Children of this dominant type are risk-takers, inventive, and flexible. They need to try out new ways of doing things. The real world for these children is the concrete, physical world, which becomes the starting point for carrying out their activities. Their ordering of the world is three dimensional, and not restricted to a step-by-step linear approach. These children are creative and love to explore and experiment as a way of learning. They like an environment in which a lot is going on and in which they are free to move about and make choices. These children often tend to get involved in the process of learning and are less concerned with the outcome.

Given these brief descriptions of the four types of learning styles developed by Gregorc, how can parents use this information?

After reading these descriptions, parents can sense if one or more of these types seems to fit how they see their child. [See Form 11 in Appendix A for a checklist to use.]

Keeping some of these characteristics in mind, parents can observe their child while doing school work and other activities at home. This will help to confirm and expand their thoughts and ideas. It will also give parents a chance to look for patterns of behavior that may fit one style more than another.

The goal is for parents to gain a better understanding of how their child learns by how he interacts with the world around him This, in turn, should help a parent better understand his child as a learner and how to help his child in the learning process. The goal is *not* to label a child as having one style or another, but to better understand the child as a learner. In doing this, it is important to keep in mind that although some children show dominance in one category, all children have characteristics from each of the four types.

In addition to parents *observing* their child relative to the four learning styles, they can talk to their child to see which style the child feels he is most like.

Several ways of gaining information about your child's strengths and patterns of learning have been highlighted in the above paragraphs. To help you use this information in developing strategies to support your child in the learning process, you are encouraged to record your observations about your child on Form 11 provided in Appendix A. Also, you may want to refer to the Resources section for additional information about Gardner's work and learning styles.

LIMITATIONS

Assuming you have identified several strengths that your child has relative to the learning process, it is time to move on to considering what limitations your child has. The identification of a child's limitations will be approached from the perspective of the demands placed on a learner to achieve academically. First, it is important to note that everyone has some limitations. It is a matter of identifying what they are and how severely they interfere with the learning process for a child.

The main focus of this section will be on the academic subjects of reading, math, and writing, as most other subjects are dependent upon reading and writing skills, and sometimes the logical thinking required in solving math problems. Grouped together, these subject areas require the child to focus on and pay attention to what is being presented, to organize the information, process it, and then put the outcome into long term memory, verbalize it, or produce it in writing.

To be successful, a child must be able to sustain attention, remember what to do, retrieve information from previous learning, and complete a given task in a certain period of time. Children may experience difficulty with any one or more of these functions. Generally, for children who have been identified as having a learning difficulty, the limitation exists at the level of processing information. Some children with learning difficulties also experience limitations in paying attention. For the child who has been diagnosed as having an Attention Deficit Hyperactivity Disorder, the limitation lies at the focusing and attention levels. For parents who have children identified as having either of these difficulties, there should be documentation on the child's assessment records or diagnostic records that identify what areas of difficulty exist for the specific child. A child's teachers will also have information regarding this issue. A parent's part becomes one of learning and understanding his child's difficulty and how to help his child be successful in learning, regardless of these limitations.

CHAPTER FIVE

CHARTING YOUR CHILD'S PROGRESS

Charting your child's learning progress is an essential part of his education. It is the part of your child's education that tells you how much your child is learning and the rate at which he is learning in all subject areas. This information gives you the opportunity to make two types of comparisons. First, you can compare your child's progress with his own past performance. Second, you can compare your child's performance to other children of the same age and grade level. In the case of children with disabilities that affect their learning, it is especially important for parents and teachers to keep in mind the progress a child makes compared to his past performance and the differences that occur among subject areas.

ABILITY, ACHIEVEMENT, AND PERFORMANCE

Collaborative efforts and communication between parents and their child's school are necessary for determining how a child is progressing in school. It is your right as a parent to know whatever the school knows about the abilities, achievements, and performance of your child. Your child's school staff has the obligation to share this information with you in an understandable way. Much of this information is communicated through your child's report card, parent/teacher conferences and your child's Individual Educational Plan. When and if you need additional information, it is the school's responsibility to comply with your request to meet with your child's educational team for this purpose.

As a part of this team, the school psychologist should also be available to discuss any of this information with you.

INFORMATION ON YOUR CHILD

Cognitive ability or **intelligence** has to do with the thinking or problem-solving abilities of your child. It is an index of your child's capacity to learn. Children have varying capacities relative to how much and how fast they can learn academic subjects. The most widely used standardized test administered individually is the Wechsler Intelligence Scale for Children. Most children (68%), when compared by age, fall within the *average* range of intellectual functioning. Of the remaining 32%, 16% fall within the *above average* range of intellectual functioning and 16% fall within the *below average* range of intellectual functioning. Where your child falls within this continuum should be reported to you as a part of your child's assessment for special education, and should be documented on your child's Individual Educational Plan.

Your child's *ability* score is used to determine his eligibility for special education. Once your child is being serviced by special education teachers, the ability score is used for setting expectations for your child's progress in learning.

Achievement tests measure what your child has learned from instruction and experience. It is what your child actually knows in any given subject at the point in time the test was given. In addition to the standardized tests given to your child in a group setting, your child was given an achievement test designed to be given on an individual basis. The Woodcock Johnson Tests of Achievement, the Kaufman Tests of Educational Achievement, and the Wechsler Individual Achievement Tests are among the most widely used individual achievement tests given at the current time.

Individual achievement tests are given to your child at the time your child is referred for an assessment to determine eligibility for special education. After your child is placed in special education, an achievement test is given every three years to determine your child's progress in reading, math, and written language. Achievement tests are compared to your child's intelligence test score to determine the degree to which your child is learning compared to the expectation for his measured intelligence. [See Form 12 in Appendix A.]

Performance is the term used to indicate how your child is doing on a day-to-day basis. This is most often determined by how your child does on daily assignments and by the observations made by your child's teachers.

The three types of information just described are primarily concerned with your child's capacity to learn and the rate at which your child is acquiring academic skills. However, to honor the perspective of the whole child, you also need to pay attention to how your child is growing and developing emotionally, socially, and physically. Not only is this necessary to keep these factors in balance with academic growth, but to recognize that there is a strong relationship between these aspects of your child and success in learning.

HOW INFORMATION IS REPORTED

Most of the information about your child's progress is reported through the use of report cards, teacher observations, your child's work samples and projects, and test scores. Each has its place in giving you as complete a picture as possible about your child. Test scores should always be used in conjunction with what you and your child's teachers know about your child's daily performance and overall achievement. They should not be interpreted in isolation or given greater credibility compared to the other types of information about your child.

Remember, any test is a sample of your child's learning behavior at a given point in time. Test scores should be compared to a child's daily work and teachers' observations to determine if there is a consistency among them. If not, the reason for the inconsistency should be explored to account for the differences.

The following information should be kept in mind when you chart your child's learning progress:

Information from Grades

Grades are generally assigned to your child on either an A-F basis or a rating basis such as Satisfactory, Needs Improvement, or Unsatisfactory. Some school districts have shifted to a mastery basis. This grading system lists the objectives a child needs to achieve and indicates whether the objective has been mastered or partially mastered.

In charting your child's progress, it is important for you to fully understand the system that is used for your child's report card. Also, you need to know if your child is on a modified marking system for specific subjects and understand how this is indicated on the report card. You can get information about the report card system used for your child by referring to the code for marking that appears on the report card and by conversing with your child's teachers. An appropriate question to ask of your child's teachers is, "*What is the basis for my child's grade?*" If your child's report card system is based on mastery ask, "*What are the criteria for mastery?*"

Information from Work Samples, Projects, etc.

If you are a parent of a younger child, it is typical to have your child bring home his completed work every day. This gives you an ongoing opportunity to see how your child is performing in specific subjects on a daily basis. It is usually in the best interests of your child if you acknowledge the completion of the task, give positive praise for what he has learned, and ask if there are questions or items he would like to go over with you. This approach to work brought home fosters confidence in your child as a learner and recognizes his efforts. To spend time going over the items missed, unless your child or his teachers ask you to, reinforces any inadequate feelings your child has. Chances are that your child's teacher has already gone over these items, so there is no need to duplicate efforts.

The purpose of your child's daily work is twofold: one, to let you know what your child is working on, and two, to give you feedback on the progress your child is making.

For parents whose child is at the secondary level, it is best to work out some arrangement with your child as to how this feedback will be communicated. A common practice at the secondary level is for teachers to notify parents if their child is doing unsatisfactory work at the half-way point of the marking period.

Information from Teachers' Observations

This information is generally shared with parents at parent/teacher conference time. Some report cards have a section for teachers to write comments based on their observations of your child. These comments focus on how your child is doing in each area of school learning, statements about your child's work habits, and any problems your child may be experiencing.

If your child is having difficulties in one or more of these areas, it is your option to set up a daily or weekly communication system with your child's teachers to get more frequent feedback. Teachers are keen observers of children, making them an invaluable source of information for parents to log on their child's progress chart. Parents are also keen observers of their children. This makes their input an equally meaningful source of information to also include on their child's progress chart. Remember, teachers have the *comparative perspective*, which is a lot of knowledge about children your child's age relative to learning and development. *You* as the parent, know your child's past history best.

STANDARDIZED TESTS

Test scores come from several sources such as teacher-made tests, text-book company tests, statewide mastery tests, and standardized tests. Even though each of these tests has value for certain purposes, our discussion will be limited to the types of scores reported from the use of standardized tests.

Standardized tests are generally objective in that the items have a right response or a set of criteria from which to objectively score responses. Standardized tests are based on how sample populations of children of varying ages and grade levels across the United States performed. Scores from stand-ardized tests, such as the Wechsler Intelligence Scale for Children, are most often reported as standard scores or percentile scores. Some achievement tests (another example of standardized tests), also use grade equivalency and age equivalency scores. Each of these scores is defined below:

Standard Scores

This way of reporting and communicating test results is the most reliable one to use. However, it is not as easy to understand as the other three types listed in this section. A standard score is a score that has been *normalized* on a group of children across age groups. A common number used to denote the midpoint of the *average* range is 100, give or take a few points for error in testing.

Any standard score that lies between 85 and 115 is considered to be within the *average* range. This includes 68% of the general population of children. Standard scores that are above 115 are considered above average and those below 85 are considered below average. Scores within these ranges can vary from somewhat above or below average to significantly above or below average.

Any test that has 100 as the midpoint of the average range and the same spread between 85 and 115, can be compared to one another. This is a distinct advantage when charting a child's progress and when needing to compare a child's score on an ability test to his score on an achievement test. This type of comparison is used to determine whether or not a child is achieving at a level that is consistent with his measured ability. For children with learning disabilities, this is one of the criteria to be considered for receiving special education services. [See Form 12 in Appendix A for an example.]

Percentile Scores

For every standard score, there is an equivalent percentile score ranging from < 1% to > 99%. Percentile scores tell you the number of children that scored above your child and the number of children who scored below your child when taking the same test. For example, if you were told your child scored at the 80% on a math test he took, it means he did as well as or better than 80% of the other children who took the same test. This also means that 20% of the children taking that test scored higher than your child. Put another way, if 100 children took this math test, your child would have scored the same or higher than 80 children and 20 children would have scored higher than your child. Given the fact that any percentile score between the 25% and the 75% is considered to be within the average range, your child's score at the 80% places him in the above average range on this math test. This means your child is doing well in math, based on this test. If, on the other hand, your child's score was at the 50% level, this means he scored at the midpoint of the average range, equivalent to a standard score of 100.

Percentile scores are easier to understand compared to standard scores, but are not as accurate statistically. A further disadvantage of percentile scores is that they cannot be statistically added together to obtain an average of several combined scores.

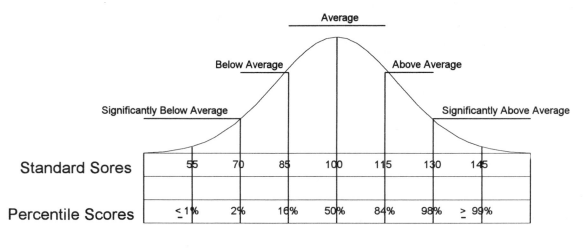

A Typical Distribution of Standard and Percentile Scores

Figure 6

Grade Equivalent Scores

Grade equivalent scores are based on the performance of typical students at each grade level. These scores are expressed as a numerical grade level and the month of that grade level ranging from September (month 1) to June (month 9). Grade equivalents seem simple and easy to understand, but serious misunderstandings may result from their use. For example, on a test given in the sixth month of the fifth year, the child with a grade equivalent of 5.6 would be performing *at grade level*. If another child in the same fifth grade classroom attains a grade equivalent score of 7.3, this does not mean this child can do seventh grade work. What it means is that this child scored as well as a typical seventh grader would have in the third month of school - *on that fifth grade test.*

In the same way, if your child attains a grade equivalent of 3.3 as a fifth grader, this does not suggest that your child has only learned material up to the third grade level. It simply means that your child did about the same as a third grader would on a fifth grade test. In other words, if your child obtains a higher grade equivalent score compared to the grade he is in, his skills are in the above average range compared to the expectation for his grade level. Similarly, if he got a grade equivalent score below the grade level he is in, his skills are below average for his grade level.

Because grade equivalents can so easily be misunderstood, their use is not recommended for the reporting of test scores. However, as many school districts report scores in this form to parents, it is important that you understand the meaning of grade equivalents. It is not recommended to use these scores when charting your child's progress. It is better to use either your child's standard scores or percentile scores, as they give you a more accurate picture of your child's academic standing and progress.

Age Equivalent Scores

Age equivalent scores are based on the performance of typical students at each age level. These scores are expressed as a numerical value by year and month of a child's age. They are similar to grade equivalent scores in that they are easy to understand, but open to misunderstanding. The use of these scores is not recommended for either ability tests or achievement tests. Also, these scores should not be used to chart your child's progress. If given these scores by your child's teacher or educational team members, ask for the equivalent standard score or percentile score.

INTERPRETING TEST SCORES

There are many cautions to consider when interpreting and charting a child's test scores. The first caution is not to use a single test or combination of test scores in isolation (as previously mentioned). A second caution has to do with the preciseness of measurement one can expect in test scores.

Since test scores are given in numbers, it is easy to interpret them as absolutes. Because of test error, testing conditions and the changing conditions of children, test scores should be interpreted as a number within a range rather than as a precise number. For example, if a child obtains a standard score of 100, his actual score could be at any point on a continuum between 95 and 105. For some tests, the range is larger than 10 points. You can obtain this information from the person who shared the test results with you. In turn, this information is important in measuring your child's progress, as growth needs to be based on a several point difference between tests; it cannot be based on a 2 to 3 point difference.

Another caution to keep in mind when interpreting test results is the reading level of the test items compared to your child's reading ability. If your child's reading ability is less than the reading level required to read the test items, the test becomes more a test of your child's reading ability than a test of his knowledge.

Children with disabilities often find taking tests difficult. They may have trouble following directions, understanding what to do, expressing their answers in writing, etc. For these children, daily performance and mastery testing on the subject matter they have been taught serve as better indicators of what they have learned.

CREATING A PROGRESS CHART

The information you have just read has been foundation material for creating a system for recording and charting your child's progress. The remainder of this chapter will focus on ways for doing this and examples of progress charts. To begin this process, you need to think about:

♦ what information you want to record and measure, i.e., your child's academic progress in each subject area, or include other information about his work completion, attitude toward each subject, emotional and social growth, etc.

♦ decide what indicators or measures to use for each type of information you decide to chart

♦ decide on the best time to start and how often you are going to record each type of information

♦ decide how you want to approach this process so that you include your child in the process

♦ decide who is going to keep the chart and where it should be kept. In the case of older children, they may want full responsibility for this.

Keep this information in mind as you look at the examples of progress charts. Then decide what will work best for you and your child. Make it a fun project for both of you. The more involved your child is, the more he will participate and take responsibility for his chartings.

Progress Chart Examples

Example 1: An Appraisal of Your Child's School Performance

	Reading Yes / No	Math Yes / No	Writing Yes / No	Art Yes / No	Science Yes / No	etc.
How I Am Doing in School Name_____ Date Completed_____						
Areas						
I am doing satisfactory work						
I complete all my assignments						
I like this subject						
(Add more as needed)						

To complete this chart: [A similar chart is provided for you as Form 13 in Appendix A.]

1) Put aside time to meet with your child to discuss the purpose of the chart and to get the information from him.

2) Fill in all the subject areas your child is currently taking across the top of the chart. Have your child write them in (or you do the recording if your child prefers) in the order in which the child thinks of them. You may add other areas of school life, such as friends, if you wish.

3) Have your child answer each question for each area by putting a check in either the **YES** or **NO** column.

4) Highlight all the **YES**'s in each column with a colored (i.e., green) highlight pen.

5) Circle the **NO**'s in pencil for each column.

6) Use your child's most recent report card and information from your child's teacher to verify your child's perceptions about how he is doing. If any of

these were inaccurate, discuss the reasons why with your child and change the response on the chart.

7) Make a list of the **NO**'s for each area on a separate sheet of paper.

8) Make a decision as to which **NO**'s are the most important to work on first. It is best to start out with no more than 2-3 areas and put the others on hold for a later time.

9) Circle the items chosen to be worked on. Have your child write a goal for each item relative to what he needs to do to move this item to the **YES** column on the original form he filled out.

10) For ease in charting, record the items and goals on a new form, such as the one below: [or use Form 14 in Appendix A.]

Areas I Will Work On					
	Goal	Week 1 Yes P No	Week 2 Yes P No	Week 3 Yes P No	etc.
Reading	Complete Assignment				
Math	Complete Assignment				
Writing	Complete Assignment				

Check your child's progress at the end of each week. If your child has achieved the goal, have him put a check in **YES** column. If he partially met his goal (3 of 5 days that week), put 3/5 in the **P** (partially met) column. If your child made no progress toward his goal, discuss ways to change his approach so he can make progress the next week.

11) As each goal is achieved, go back to the original chart, have your child erase the appropriate **NO** check, put a check in the **YES** column and highlight it with green.

12) Repeat this process until all the **NO** checks have been erased and all checks are in the **YES** column highlighted by a green marker. It is important to praise your child on completion of each goal. When the chart is all green (or mostly green), have a special celebration with your child.

13) Each time your child receives his report card, start with # 1, revising and updating the information on your child's school performance as needed.

Example 2: Charting Your Child's Standardized Test Scores

Plot your child's most recent test scores on a chart similar to the following one: [Refer to Form 15 in Appendix A.]

Standardized Test Scores for <u>Jerry</u>

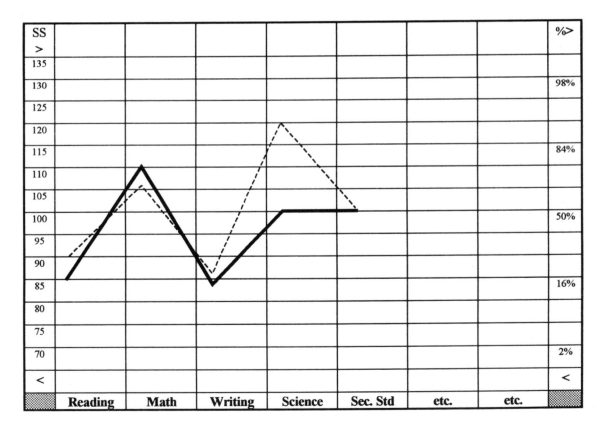

Jerry, a fourth grade child, obtained the following standard scores:

	September, 1994	June, 1995
Reading	85	90
Math	110	106
Writing	84	87
Science	100	120
Soc. Studies	100	102

Jerry's scores have been plotted on the above graph.

What do these two sets of test scores mean in relation to Jerry's academic progress (as measured by standardized tests) for the 1994-1995 school year? As recorded on the graph, the scores between the two sets of tests were all within (+) or (-) 5 points of each other except in science. This means that Jerry made exceptional progress in science compared to other children who took the same test and satisfactory progress in all the rest of the subject areas. The fact that his second set of test scores were similar to his first set, means he maintained a satisfactory rate of acquiring skills in those areas compared to his peers. If, in the second set of test scores, he had received a significantly lower score in any area, a follow-up would be necessary with Jerry's teachers to determine the consistency of the lower score with his daily performance. If inconsistent, the test score is most likely not reflecting the skills Jerry has acquired. If the score is consistent with his performance, an analysis of why Jerry is not making sufficient progress in that subject area should be performed.

For your child, record each set of test scores in a different color. Be sure to date each set of test scores. This type of chart will then give you a graphic representation of your child's progress as measured by standardized test scores.

The above examples of charts can be used in the format they are given, or adapted to fit your child's needs.

[Refer to Forms 13, 14, and 15 in Appendix A for copies of each chart.]

CHAPTER SIX

CREATING A HOME ENVIRONMENT FOR LEARNING

Children at school, when engaged in the learning process, are expected to follow routines and complete assignments within certain time limits. Parents need to encourage routines and reasonable expectations for assignments or special projects at home. Parents are the key to enhancing the learning success of their children.

There are many aspects for parents to think about in providing appropriate learning environments for their children in the home setting. There is the physical space in which the child does the work and there are materials the child needs to have available and organized to do the various tasks. Times to work on the task need to be defined, and how a parent can best be involved with his child during learning times needs to be a consideration.

WORK SPACE

All children, regardless of age or learning style, need to have a designated space set aside for doing their school assignments at home. It is best to have this space away from any traffic pattern of the household and separate from other members of the family. If a child has attention difficulties and is easily distracted by what he sees or hears, this is a must. If your child helps to choose the location and atmosphere of this study space, he will take more responsibility for making this space a successful place of work. In the case of older children, it is best for them to do the choosing and planning of their work space themselves, as long as it is reasonable for the rest of the family and produces appropriate results.

Once the space is designated, let your child (with your help, in the case of younger children), plan how to best utilize the space and organize the materials needed for completing assignments and projects at home.

WORK MATERIALS

Work is done more easily and in less time if all the materials needed to do the task are available and organized. Younger children generally bring home a list of materials needed at school one of the first few days of the new school year. These are basically the same materials your child will need for completing assignments at home. [See Form 16 in Appendix A for a suggested list of materials.] Older children know what they need and can make a list to see if they have all of these materials in their study area. In either case, given a list of the materials needed, let your child make choices as to color, kind, etc. for each item. Also, take your child with you when you shop for these materials. If possible, take each of your children independently to shop, to make it a special event. The more you can do to help your child take ownership of his study space and materials, the more your child can take responsibility for his learning.

WORK TIME

Setting aside a specific time for doing homework is advisable. This, along with a specific space, helps cue a child's brain into the expectation for school work. The time set aside for homework will vary among children. Some children do best if they do it as soon as they come home from school. Others can work better if they have a break from their school day and do their homework after dinner. Occasionally, a child prefers to get up earlier in the morning and do homework before going to school. If your child attends a child care setting after school, the best time could be between dinner and bedtime.

Discuss all the possibilities with your child. Use your child's ideas in making a decision about the best time to set aside for homework. For some families, this time can be relatively consistent. For other families, the time will change depending upon the schedules of other family members. To help make study time a routine for your child, it is best to have a weekly written schedule that designates the block of time that will be set aside for homework each day. [See Form 17 in Appendix A.] If a child has no homework on a particular day, encourage your child to spend some time (varies by age) reading a book, having a story read by you, or engaging in some other type of thinking activity. How long should your child work at any one time? The length of time for homework is dependent upon your child's age. Younger children can be expected to work within a range of twenty minutes to forty-five minutes. Older children can be expected to work two or more hours steadily once they reach the high school level.

The time block for homework is also dependent upon the total amount of homework your child brings home. If your child is in kindergarten or first grade, very little homework will be assigned. If your child brings home a lot of homework at these grade levels, it is best to check with your child's teachers to see how your child is using his time in school.

From third grade on, the amount of homework continues to be dependent upon how your child uses his time in school, but also on the rate at which your child processes information, and the philosophy of your school system regarding the amount of time that should be spent doing homework for each grade level. However, there are two situations which you should check out:

1) if your child brings no homework home, and
2) if your child has to spend an excessive amount of time doing homework based on age and grade level guidelines.

INDIVIDUALIZING YOUR CHILD'S LEARNING ENVIRONMENT

The unique learning needs that emerge as a result of your child's disability are documented in your child's Individual Educational Plan provided by your child's school. You should find it helpful to refer to this plan to gain ideas for adapting your child's work space at home, to help organize your child's materials, and to plan your child's work time. You can supplement the information on your child's Individual Educational Plan by consulting with your child's teachers and educational team.

Children who have one or more disabilities generally have more difficulty in attending, organizing, planning, and using their time appropriately and efficiently compared to their peers. Therefore, it is important to find out what your child's unique learning needs are in each of these areas.

The following are questions to help you do this.

Work Space

1) How quiet and free of distraction should the work space be? Is there a need for your child's work space to be in the quietest part of the house?

2) Should your child's work space consist of anything but a desk or table to work on, an appropriate chair to sit on, adequate lighting, and the materials needed to work with?

3) Who should have access to your child's work space?

Organization of Materials

4) What is the best way to have your child organize his materials based on what works best in the school setting?

5) What additional materials or aids will your child need due to his disability to help in learning and completing assignments?

Time Block

6) What time of day works best for your child to do his homework?

7) How much time should your child be expected to spend on homework each day? In which subject areas?

8) What is the longest period of time your child can work before taking a break?

9) What is the best way to help your child prioritize his assignments - difficult to easy, easy to difficult?

10) Will your child need more time to complete assignments than the average child his age? If so, how should assignments be adapted to keep homework time within reasonable limits?

[See Form 18 in Appendix A for a way to record your ideas.]

If your child has an observable or documented learning style, there are unique learning needs that will emerge as a result of this style. These needs can be interfaced with the needs that emerged as a result of your child's disability. (Refer to Chapter 4 for the characteristics associated with the different learning styles).

Sequential learners, **concrete sequential** learners, **abstract sequential** learners, and **verbal** learners learn best when they have:

♦ a quiet, predictable environment to work in

♦ materials and study area organized neatly

♦ time lines to follow that are clearly stated

♦ an understanding of what to do and how to do it

♦ procedures for learning organized in a step-by-step manner

♦ assignments in which they can think and problem solve in words

♦ the use of lists, charts, outlines, and worksheets in their assignments

♦ consistency and structure in their learning environment

♦ consistency in expectations

♦ a goal to work toward

♦ a situation in which they can work alone

♦ a reward system and/or approval for the work they do

Simultaneous learners, **concrete random** learners, **abstract random** learners and **visual** learners learn best when they have:

♦ an environment that allows for flexibility and choice

♦ materials accessible, but having a choice for organizing them by color, shape, function, etc.

♦ blocks of time to work in which there are built-in breaks

♦ the "big picture" of what they are to do

♦ several pieces of information available to them at one time

♦ encouragement to make mental pictures of verbal information

♦ the opportunity to use pictures, charts, maps and other visual aids to use in thinking and problem solving

♦ a chance to make choices from two or more options

♦ flexibility in how they arrive at an answer or outcome

♦ the opportunity to share what they are doing with another person

♦ the opportunity to work with others

[A list of these strategies is given on Form 19 in Appendix A.]

OTHER CONSIDERATIONS

The attitude in which your child approaches the learning task can either contribute to or interfere with your child's learning success. This is especially important when your child has a disability. Having a disability generally means having to put more effort into learning to achieve the same results as someone else.

To help your child create a positive attitude about learning, you can teach your child a process by which he can approach his task. This process contains the following steps.

Step 1.

Before your child begins working on an assignment have your child say two or three positive statements about his ability to learn.
General statements may include:

- I can learn.

- I am able to do this work.

- I will remember what I am learning now.

- I can think clearly.

- I will be successful in doing this.

- I feel good about myself as a learner.

More specific statements may include:

- I can learn these _____ (colors, words, facts, etc.).

- I will know how to _____ (spell, write, say) these _____ (letters, numbers, words, etc.).

- I will finish this _____ (assignment, model, etc.) successfully.

Step 2.

Have your child formulate a statement about what it is he is to learn or do in the next 30 minutes, or whatever time is appropriate for the age of the child and the task to be accomplished.

Step 3.

Have the child translate the words of this statement into a mental picture (a picture inside his head).

Step 4.

Have your child take a few minutes (with eyes closed) to relax by breathing deeply and rhythmically while mentally picturing himself successfully completing the task.

Step 5.

Have your child begin the task with the intention of completing it successfully.

Step 6.

If your child experiences stress or "blocks" while doing the task, have the child repeat positive statements about his ability to learn. You may want to have your child add such statements as: "It is okay to make mistakes while I am learning," and/or "This will get easier for me with more practice." Also, you may have your child listen to music, relax a few minutes, and again picture himself doing the task successfully. Some children are able to concentrate better if soothing music is playing in the background. Classical music is often used for this purpose.

Step 7.

After the time block or task is completed, *secure* your child's success by having the child summarize what he accomplished and the feelings connected with the experience. Emphasize the feelings that help your child feel good about learning. Have your child repeat this process each time before beginning an assignment. Eventually, your child will be able to follow this procedure on his own, automatically.

Note: These steps may be adjusted in any way that works best for you and your child. The purpose in going through this type of process is to facilitate learning. This happens when children feel good about themselves as learners and are relaxed, allowing them to utilize all of their resources. This, in turn, results in being able to focus and concentrate on the learning at hand.

ENCOURAGEMENT AND INDEPENDENCE

Children tend to feel more competent about themselves as learners if they feel they can rely on their own resources to complete assignments. This means that your child needs to develop as much independence as a learner as is appropriate for his age. To do this, your child needs encouragement given when you, by your words and actions, reinforcing the fact that your child *can* learn. The words used to convey this message to your child are perhaps more easily given than actions, particularly when you observe your child getting frustrated and discouraged over an assignment. When this happens, reinforce your child's belief that he can be successful, work through the situation together, and encourage your child to try the new solutions the next time a problem is encountered.

Continuous reinforcement of your child's abilities to learn and teaching your child how to get through frustrating times will result in your child feeling more confident that he is capable as a learner and has many resources *within himself* to solve problems. Independence developed during your child's earlier years of school will carry over to the later years when your child reaches the secondary grades. Encouraging your child's independence as a learner is also a way to encourage your child to take ownership of his learning and responsibility for completing assigned tasks.

Children also need to get feedback from you about how they are doing. In giving this feedback, it is better to call attention to what the child has accomplished rather than what was left incomplete or done incorrectly. Then, together with your child, decide on a goal for next time.

Creating a positive learning environment at home for your child is both a challenge and an opportunity. It is a challenge from the standpoint of creating an environment that will support your child's success in learning. It is an opportunity to better know and understand your child as a person and as a learner. It is also an opportunity for you to work closely with your child's teachers and educational team with the focus of providing the best possible learning environments for your child.

"Every child," says Gardner Murphy in his book, Personality, "is in some ways like all other children. In some ways he is like some other children. And in some ways, he is like no other child." Herein lies our challenge and opportunity, to discover the uniqueness of each child and to provide the experiences that will address this uniqueness.

CHAPTER SEVEN

STRATEGIES FOR HELPING YOUR CHILD WITH HOMEWORK

Children need varying amounts of help with their homework. Our responsibility as parents is to give them the amount of help they need, but not to overdo it. The help they need may take many forms. It can be given in the form of emotional support and encouragement, as well as given directly in the form of help with specific subjects. The focus here will be on strategies parents can use with their children when helping them in the areas of reading, math, written language, and attention.

Parents are not expected to be their child's school teacher. What your child will need from you is occasional help to get him through a problem he does not quite understand. This is a follow-up to the teaching that took place for your child at school. You act as a reinforcer of this teaching.

It is in your child's best interests that you have an overview of what is being taught at your child's grade level. This information is often communicated in writing from your child's teachers at the beginning of each school year. Some school districts offer a "curriculum night" in which parents can get this information.

It is also important for you to know what modifications are being made for your child as a result of his disability. These modifications may be relative to the expectations set for your child, the content of subject matter, assignments, grading, and taking tests. Your child will benefit more from your help if there is a consistency between home and school around these issues.

As you work with your child, always give the message, in both words and actions, that he is a capable learner. It is important that your child understand his disability (the degree of understanding varies with age), but also know he *can* learn, sometimes in the same way as other children, and sometimes in different ways. Your child may need to be reminded of this repeatedly until he gets to the point of believing it.

Emphasizing strengths is another way to help build your child's confidence as a learner. Overemphasis on your child's disability can lead a child to generalize his disability to the point of feeling that learning is too hard and something out of his reach. Your positive involvement in your child's learning and homework is a key to his success as a learner and how he feels about himself as a learner.

GENERAL GUIDELINES

Positive involvement can be based on general guidelines as you help your child with his homework, and strategies when working with your child on specific subjects. Each of these will be addressed separately.

First, here are some general guidelines to keep in mind.

1) Always have your child work in his "designated" place for doing homework.

2) Encourage your child to approach the task with a positive attitude.

3) Check to see if your child understands what to do. Have your child verbalize this or show you his homework notebook.

4) Check to see if your child understands how to do the assignment. Have him explain it to you or show you.

5) Have your child check to see if he has all the necessary materials in his work space to complete the assignments he will be working on.

6) Review the procedure for your child to ask you for help.

7) Have your child tell you what he needs to accomplish during this homework time. If your child has more than one assignment, have your child prioritize which task to approach first, second, etc.

8) Reinforce the idea to your child that he is a capable learner and can complete the assigned work successfully.

9) Remind your child that he can ask you for help and then leave him alone in his work space.

Note: These guidelines can be adapted so that they are comfortable for you, and so that they correctly correspond to the age of your child.

HELPING WITH READING

Reading is a complex process which places many demands on the child. Learning to read involves visual and auditory processing functions, associative functions, integrative functions, sequencing functions, memory functions, and motor functions. Initially, these functions are required to learn to read and later to access information through reading. When you help your child with reading, it is not necessary to fully understand each of these functions. However, being aware of the complexity of the reading process as you work with your child can give you some clues for ways you can help your child.

To make these functions more understandable, a brief explanation of each function follows:

Visual processing.
Involves taking in information visually and giving meaning to it. The first phase of reading is a visual process - seeing letters, words, and sentences in printed form.

Auditory processing.
Involves taking in information that is given verbally and making sense of it. In reading, all letters and groups of letters are assigned specific sounds and sound combinations. Reading orally and listening to stories involves auditory processing. All directions given verbally are dependent upon auditory processing.

Associative functions.

Seeing how things go together. In reading, this is making associations between letters and their sounds, and printed words and their meaning. It also covers how previous learning fits with current learning.

Integrative functions.

Combining one or more functions together, such as the integration of visual and auditory functions, eye and motor functions, etc. Reading initially involves attaching sounds to visual symbols in order to read the printed word. It also involves putting down on paper what you have read or reproducing in writing what you have seen.

Sequencing.

Organizing and putting letters, words, sentences, etc. in correct order. Reading is very dependent on sequencing functions. Most sequencing functions are, in turn, dependent upon memory.

Memory.

Required for the recall and storage of all learning. All aspects of reading are dependent upon visual and auditory memory as well as immediate, intermediate, and long-term memory.

Motor development.

Motor development of the eyes is involved in reading words and sentences in sequence. Eye/hand coordination is involved in writing letters, words, sentences, etc.

Children who have difficulty learning to read and accessing information by reading have difficulty in one or more of these functions. The greater the degree of severity of a child's disability, the greater the likelihood of having processing difficulties in multiple functions. In cases of severe disability, a parent's primary task is to help keep the child motivated to learn. For this child, many tasks are arduous and discouragingly difficult to carry out at home. For more information about your child relative to these functions and the degree of disability present, refer to your child's Individual Educational Plan and consult with your child's educational team.

STRATEGIES TO USE WITH EACH READING FUNCTION

If your child's disability includes difficulties in visual processing:

1) Encourage your child to translate visual material into words. Have your child think in words and express these aloud as he is working.

2) When your child encounters a new word, have him try to say the word by sounding each part out rather than trying to recall the word from its pattern or visual image.

3) Encourage your child to recall previously learned words by making auditory images of the word. This involves remembering the sequence of sounds rather than seeing the sequence of letters in the word.

4) Have your child highlight letters and combinations of letters with different colors to help your child pay visual attention to the letters in a word.

5) Help your child observe the visual details of reading by verbalizing what letters and words look like and which sounds go with each letter and combination of letters.

6) While reading a story, when encountering a new word have your child use the context of the phrase or paragraph to help access the meaning of the word. The context is the idea expressed by the words around the unfamiliar word.

If your child's disability includes difficulties in auditory processing:

1) Reduce the amount of verbal explanations you use when working with your child. Shift as much as you can to demonstrating or showing your child what to do. An example or model of what something should look like when completed can be especially helpful for your child.

2) Slow down your rate of talking when explaining something to your child. Pause more often and emphasize important information by changing your tone of voice.

3) Use pictures and visual cues simultaneously with verbal material as much as possible.

4) Exclude as much background noise as possible when your child is working on his homework. TV should not be on if it is within your child's hearing distance while he is working.

5) If your child needs help reading a story or information for science, social studies, etc., you can assist by reading the sentences aloud while your child reads the same sentences to himself. If needed, have the child read each sentence after you have read a sentence.

6) Be alert to whether your child gains a greater understanding of the material when reading aloud or when reading silently.

7) Encourage your child to access new information by pictures first, then words, as pictures will often help give a child an initial understanding about the content of the information.

8) Encourage your child to make mental pictures as he is reading words to describe something or tell a story. Making mental pictures helps a child cue into the words and also gain a greater understanding of what is being said in words.

If your child's disability includes difficulties in associative and integrative functions:

1) Help your child link new information to familiar knowledge. The use of imagery is an effective way to encourage your child do this, either auditorially or visually or by combining the two.

2) Help your child make associations between what he hears or sees with an action that might follow.

3) Simultaneously use pictures and words to help your child understand a new idea.

4) Have your child listen to text on a tape recorder while following along in a book. This helps your child hear and see the text simultaneously.

5) Use an approach called *shadow reading* when helping your child access information through reading. This involves you and your child reading together. You read simultaneously with your child, and when your child is reading confidently, you allow your voice to fade away to a shadow. Whenever your child falters, your voice comes in more strongly and maintains the pace, fading again as the child gains confidence. Continue this pattern as long as your child needs it. By this approach, your child at all times both sees the printed words and hears them pronounced correctly. This method also helps your child read more smoothly.

6) Have your child use a technique called *RAP* when he is reading a story or a textbook for content. The acronym *RAP* stands for:

> **R**ead the paragraph.
> **A**sk yourself to recall the main idea and several details about what you have read.
> **P**lace the main ideas and important details into your own words.

If your child's disability includes difficulty in one or more types of memory such as immediate, intermediate, long-term, visual, or auditory memory:

1) When working with your child, control the amount of new information that your child has to deal with. Help your child break his work into small segments and review what he has done before going to the next segment of work.

2) Encourage your child to use imagery as a learning tool to help him remember and recall information already learned. For example, when memorizing that the freezing point of water is 32 degrees Fahrenheit, your child can imagine an ice cube or frozen lake next to the number 32.

3) Have your child make flash cards of important facts he will need to know for future learning. Have your child review the facts at home before the new learning dependent upon these facts is introduced at school. Encourage your child to spend a few minutes each day reviewing these facts. To make

practice more fun, make duplicates of the flash cards and play the game *Concentration* with them.

4) Link or relate learning to the life experiences of your child. Your child will retain information better if it is meaningful to him. It also may make the recalling of information easier for your child.

5) Introduce your child to the use of mnemonics to assist his memory. Mnemonics is the process of creating rhymes, stories, acronyms, pictures, etc. to help your memory retain and recall information. The rhymes, etc. can be as outlandish and irrational as your child wishes to make them.

If your child's disability includes difficulties in oculo-motor (eye movements) or eye/hand coordination, both aspects of motor development, here are some suggestions to improve his learning skills:

1) If your child has trouble keeping his place on a page while reading, encourage the use of a bookmark for placement on the line being currently read or help your child make a *window* to use for reading. A *window* consists of a stiff piece of paper (large index card works well) in which a slot has been cut out. The slot can be large enough to expose one word at a time, several words, or a whole line, depending upon your child's optimal eye span. As your child gains better control over his eye movements, the visual span may be gradually increased by enlarging the size of the window to include more than one line of text.

2) Consult with your eye doctor to determine if your child can increase control over his eye movements by doing prescribed exercises.

HELPING WITH WRITING

Writing is part of the reading process whenever your child needs to put information on paper. This occurs most when your child is required to answer in written form rather than verbal form, to do worksheets to practice the skills associated with reading, to do a written summary of a story, etc. Even though writing is an integral part of the reading process, the strategies for difficulties in motor development relating to eye/hand coordination will be covered in the next section.

Children encounter difficulties in writing for several reasons. However, the primary reasons are due to delays in small-motor development and difficulties in expressing ideas in written form. If your child's disabilities include delays in small-motor development:

1) Help your child create a pencil grip out of adhesive tape for his pencil. If you prefer, you can purchase one at an office supply store.

2) Check with your child's teacher as to the size of the lined paper that works best for your child. Have your child work on the same size paper at home.

3) Provide an alphabet card or letter line at your child's work space so he can see how each letter is made.

4) Regardless of your child's age, be flexible in allowing your child to either print or use cursive when working on assignments. A child generally knows which is the most efficient for him.

5) When your child needs to write a creative story or report, let him dictate the story to you so that his thoughts and ideas do not get lost in the mechanics of writing. Check with your child's teacher to see if the completed story or report needs to be re-copied before turning it in. In either case, your child should be given credit for the *quality* of his ideas, not necessarily his expression through writing.

6) When appropriate, encourage your child to learn to do his written assignments on computer.

If your child's disability includes difficulties in expressing himself on paper:

1) Before writing, have your child draw a picture to illustrate what he is going to be writing about. Then have your child start finding words to verbally describe what is in the picture. From there, have your child write the words into sentences and paragraphs.

2) Help or encourage your child to create a word bank (a list of words that are associated with a particular topic). Then have your child use this word bank to generate ideas for sentences to fit the topic.

3) Encourage your child to keep a collection of pictures available from which he can get ideas.

4) Develop a series of questions to help your child generate and organize his thoughts.

5) Have your child work from an outline for his story or topic.

6) Use *mind mapping* or *webbing* as a technique for your child to use when he needs to write a story or a report. This technique involves starting with a theme or topic as a central point and then elaborating on that point using words or phrases that refer back to that topic. [See Figure 9.] After doing this process, a child is better prepared to express his ideas in sentence and paragraph form.

[For examples other than Figure 9, see Form 20 in Appendix A.]

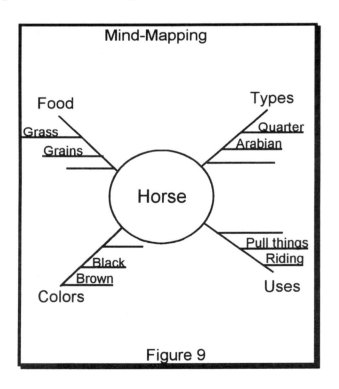

Figure 9

7) Have your child *tell* you what thoughts and ideas he has for his story. having put thoughts and ideas into *verbal* form, it is easier to translate these thoughts and ideas into *written* form.

8) Whenever appropriate for the assignment and the expectations of your child's teacher, encourage your child to use alternative ways to share his knowledge. This could include making a video of the information, making a display, giving a talk, doing a demonstration, or making a model.

<u>HELPING WITH MATH</u>

Visual processing difficulties have a greater influence on the learning of mathematics than reading. Understanding visual relationships through the use of numbers is essential to math. Rote memory, required to memorize math facts, is also important for speed and efficiency in making math calculations.

Adequate eye-hand coordination is necessary for the accurate placement of numbers and columns of numbers as well as for the legibility of numbers, to prevent unnecessary mistakes in calculation. Most math problems require multiple, sequential steps in order to produce correct answers.

If your child's disability includes difficulties in one or more of the above areas or other areas that impact the learning of math:

1) Have your child use a number line up to the number 30 on his table or desk to refer to for the correct way to write numbers and for the correct sequence of numbers.

2) Have your child have a box of small objects such as chips available in his workspace to use as counters when first learning the meaning of numbers. He can also use these for simple calculations before doing the problem on paper or to check his work.

3) Help your child attach personal meaning to math problems by giving examples of how math is used for different things in the home (its use in shopping, etc.).

4) Have your child use lined paper in a vertical rather than horizontal position (or graph paper) to help with the placement of numbers, if that is a problem for your child.

5) If your child has great difficulty copying math problems, check with your child's teacher to see if you can get a consumable math book for your child. This is a book in which the child can write, without having to duplicate the math problem on another sheet of paper.

6) Provide visual models of completed math problems for your child. Be sure the model clearly shows all of the steps needed for the solution of that type of problem.

7) Have your child construct a matrix of multiplication tables to keep in his workspace if he is having difficulty memorizing these.

8) Have your child make flash cards for the facts he is having difficulty remembering. These should be reviewed at least once a day.

9) Check to see if your child understands some of the basic words used in math such as: same, different, equal, more, less, etc. If your child does not easily comprehend some of these, have him work with objects of different colors, sizes, etc. until he understands what the concepts mean when doing math problems.

10) Check with your child's teacher regarding the use of a calculator for your child if your child has spent more than adequate time trying to memorize math facts, but having very little success.

11) If your child has difficulty changing from one kind of problem (addition to subtraction, etc.) while working on a series of problems, have your child glance through the worksheet and circle all the addition signs, subtraction signs, etc, in different colors before starting to solve the problems. This will call your child's attention to what process to use in solving each problem.

HELPING WITH ATTENTION PROBLEMS

Learning is dependent on paying attention. First, it involves focusing on the initial instruction that precedes any new learning, and second, it involves sustaining attention long enough to complete a task. Children who have been diagnosed as having an Attention Deficit Disorder have a very difficult time with both initial attention and sustaining attention. Other children without this disorder may also experience some of these difficulties, but not to the same degree.

Medication is often prescribed to help the child with an Attention Deficit Disorder. However, these children, along with the 25% who do not respond positively to medication, will need additional interventions to help them focus and learn. The following are some interventions and strategies parents can use at home to assist their children in completing their homework.

1) Whenever you speak to your child, be sure he has eye contact with you and appears to be ready to listen.

2) Help your child break tasks into shorter segments, allowing for more frequent breaks compared to the expectations for other children of similar age. A written schedule of work time and breaks will help structure this for your child.

3) Remind your child to have his work area free of visual distractions. Your child's workspace should be clear except for the materials needed for the immediate assignment.

4) Be sure all auditory distractions have been reduced as much as possible.

5) Have your child organize and label all his materials needed for homework into sections based on subject.

6) Have your child use different colored folders for keeping the homework papers for each subject.

7) Use a timer to help keep your child on task and working for the appropriate amount of time. Tell him ahead of time what he is to do during the time interval and then set the timer for a period of time that matches his attention

abilities. If he engages in behavior that is incompatible with academic work, stop the timer, tell him what he *should* be doing, and reset the timer.

8) Encourage your child to think beyond the first answer that *pops* into his head. Often a second response is of better quality when your child is impulsive.

9) Encourage your child to *talk* himself through rote tasks, such as solving math problems or writing letters, to help decrease impulsiveness and keep focused.

10) Present homework assignments and worksheets one at a time, rather than all at once. Upon completion of each assignment or worksheet, briefly check it and voice your approval before giving him the next one to work on.

11) Encourage the use of a homework notebook which contains two pocket folders: **Work To Be Done** (includes all homework, papers to be signed, etc.), and **Completed Work** (includes all completed work and signed papers to be returned to school). Your child should tape his assignment sheet on the inside of the notebook.

12) Check with your child's teacher to see if he can keep an extra set of books at home if your child repeatedly forgets to bring home the books necessary for completing his homework.

   In addition to the these strategies, many parents are getting positive results by paying attention to their child's diet, the amount of television their child watches, and their child's sleep patterns.

NUTRITION

   Nutrition has been found to be a factor in improving a child's concentration at school and at home. The effects of sugar and food additives in a child's diet have been found to increase the child's activity level, sometimes making him hyperactive, which can interfere with a child's ability to listen and concentrate in general, as well as with school work. Decreasing the ingestion of these substances has been shown to have a positive effect on learning, as well as on behavior. Good nutrition provided at regular intervals can assist the child's body to regulate itself in a steady, even manner, allowing the child's physical body to act as a support rather than a detriment to the learning process.

Adding vitamin and mineral supplements to the child's diet can often have a positive effect on how a child feels physically, which results in good attendance and more energy to put into the learning process.

SLEEP PATTERNS

Parents can help their child by paying attention to their child's sleep patterns and the quality of sleep the child gets.

A child's sleep pattern is an important indicator of how much sleep and the quality of sleep a child gets. Restful sleep is an essential part of a child's ability to pay attention and concentrate on learning while awake.

Children who have trouble falling asleep at night, sleep intermittently, or do not sleep in a relaxed state have difficulty re-energizing their bodies for the next day's activities. If this becomes a chronic problem, often memory, thinking, and concentration skills are diminished. If these problems persist, talk to your child about possible causes. These problems must be resolved *before* other disability issues can be successfully addressed.

EXCESS STIMULI

Decreasing the amount of stimuli and distractions in the home can have a calming effect on children. Cutting down on the amount of time a child spends watching television, and carefully selecting what the child watches are ways to reduce the amount of stimuli in the home. Computer and television monitors both emit large amounts of radiation, which serves to overstimulate the viewer. Replacing television viewing time with relaxing music, or perhaps with creative family activities, will not only create a more inclusive atmosphere within the home environment for the child, but also a more calming one. This will, in essence, synchronize the entire family to the same pace, and all will calm down in the process.

The strategies outlined in this chapter are meant to serve only as suggestions. As you work with your child, you will undoubtedly discover additional strategies. Encourage your child to think of new ways to approach his homework. It is important to get feedback from your child as to which strategies work best for him. Let your child take on as much responsibility as he is capable in applying these strategies. Support your child in his efforts and give as much positive, genuine praise as you can for both effort and accomplishment.

[See Form 21 in Appendix A for suggested words and phrases to use.]

CHAPTER EIGHT

EXPERIENCES AND INSIGHTS

Experiences often provide us with invaluable insights that lead to better ways of performing. These insights, in turn, help us create new visions of what is needed in our work and in the rest of our lives. This chapter will review some of the experiences and insights I have gained over the past several years as a psychologist, a counselor, a teacher, and most importantly, as a parent.

PARENTS' QUESTIONS

In my work as a school psychologist, the most frequently asked question by parents having a child with a disability is, "Will my child outgrow the conditions of the disability and "catch up" with his peers at some point in his school career?"

There is no single or universal answer to this question. The rate of academic progress a child with a disability can make is dependent upon many factors, the most prominent being the cause and conditions associated with the disability, and the severity of the disability. It is also dependent upon the success of the interventions of the special education services provided by the school and the amount of involvement of the parents in their child's educational development.

The answer to this question is further complicated by the fact that any one disability plays out differently for each child. Although there are commonalities with other children having similar disabilities, each child's disability is unique.

These factors interact to form the basis of a child's progress. The success of the child's learning is the result of what the child brings into the situation and how the environment (parent, school staff, friends, etc.) responds to the child. All of these elements combined make it extremely difficult, if not impossible, to make any kind of prediction as to whether a child can and/or will "catch up." This is especially true for children who have been diagnosed as having a learning disability, language impairment, attention deficit disorder, or emotional/ behavioral disorder. For children who have multiple disabilities, limited intelligence, or severe disabilities, the possibility of "catching up" is not likely. However, because there are so many influential factors interacting, it is extremely difficult to predict how far a child will go in his learning.

Maximum progress can be made when the child is motivated to learn, and when the home and school actively work together for the benefit of the child. Intervention at the point the child first needs it is also a key factor.

It is in the child's best interest that we do not give a definitive answer to the "Will he ever catch up?" question. Instead, both parents and educators need to focus on what the child *can* do and chart the child's progress from that starting point. It serves no purpose to make a prediction that either *over*estimates or *under*estimates what a child can do. The most productive position is to take the child at his present level and plan interventions that will optimize the development of the child's capabilities. Just as it is important not to hold unrealistic expectations for a child, it is also imperative that we not give up on any child.

An example comes to mind of a boy named Jon who had rather severe memory and associative function difficulties. He was a non-reader until fourth grade. Every possible method of teaching reading was tried, but to no avail. Although Jon tested in the upper limits of the average range of intellectual functioning, he had been diagnosed with a learning disability in reading and written language toward the end of first grade.

The dynamics that ultimately led toward the success of Jon included an excellent relationship between a special education teacher and an involved mother, and their belief that Jon could learn to read. They worked together, along with Jon's regular education teachers, continually exploring alternative ways of teaching Jon how to read. At the beginning of fourth grade, Jon started making progress in reading. At the mid-point of fourth grade, Jon stopped by my office to tell me that he "finally got the hang of reading." From that point on, he made steady progress. By end of tenth grade, his achievement in reading was consistent within the range of expectation for his measured ability, and he no longer needed the support of special education services.

Another frequently asked question by parents who have a child with a learning disability is "Should my child consider college?" or "Is college out of the question for my child?" Any child who has intellectual ability within the average range or above, who has the desire and motivation to succeed, and who needs a college education to fulfill his career goals, should look at college as an option. Many colleges and universities have a center on the college campus that is designed to meet with and support the student who has a learning disability. [See bibliography for more information.] Modifications can often be made to course requirements to accommodate the needs of these students. Students with learning disabilities can also be given special consideration for the conditions under which they take college entrance exams, such as the SAT's.

Parents who have a child with limited intelligence and/or multiple disabilities often ask, "Can the IQ (intelligence) score for my child change?" The type of intelligence the parent is referring to in this case is what we consider to be intelligence for academic learning.

Applying these factors to the question regarding whether an intelligence test score can change for a child, the answer would have to be based on the age of the child when the test was given, how the child responded to the test, and whether the test was an adequate sample of that child's thinking abilities. These guidelines should be used in viewing a child's intelligence score, which is a *general* estimate of a child's potential for learning academic subjects.

Test scores are less reliable and less stable for younger children than for older children. For pre-school children, this testing is less reliable than for older children; for children 5 through 8 years old, the score becomes more reliable; and for children 9 and older, the score will remain within a range of 5 points on either side of an actual score 90% of the time. This is due to the fact that younger children go through various developmental stages and rates of growth that continually influence their learning abilities. For this reason, it is often difficult to rely on the testing done over any one short period of time. Also, there are only a limited number of test items that can be given to young children, so the sample of behavior tends to be more limited than it is for older children.

Exceptions to these guidelines may occur in cases where a child has a severe language deficit or severe limitations in visual/spatial abilities that are the result of delayed development at the time of testing. In these cases, changes that exceed the 5 point variance on either side of an actual score are due to the growth that has taken place as a result of an increased ability for verbal expression or an increased ability to manipulate objects. Most often this occurs between the ages of 6 and 10.

There is one caution in comparing intelligence test scores given at different times to a child. Be sure that the tests to be compared are the same. Do not compare two different intelligent tests, such as the Wechsler Intelligence Scale for Children and the Kaufman Assessment Battery for Children, as they measure different aspects of problem-solving ability.

REFLECTIONS

Over the past several years, there have been many changes in regular education and special education, some more productive than others. However, there are two core beliefs that underlie the success or failure of any change. One is that the change is made for the benefit of the child rather than for the benefit of the institution or any group within the institution. The second is that we hold the belief that all children have strengths, and even though a particular child's progress may be slow, we can never give up on that child. When a child does not make progress, we need to continually search for ways to help the child learn. The question we need to ask ourselves is, "Why is this approach not working for this child?" rather than "What is wrong with the child?"

One of the most powerful ways of teaching children social skills and age-appropriate behaviors is through the use of *modeling* the behaviors that are desirable for the child. Inclusion provides a setting for all children to observe age-appropriate social skills and behaviors being modeled in a natural setting. Adjustments can be made for the learning needs of children with disabilities in this setting with the cooperative efforts of regular classroom teachers, special education teachers, administrators and additional support staff.

During my years in education, I saw many examples that demonstrated the positive effects that this modeling can have for children with disabilities. This included children with a number of different types of disabilities and severity of disabilities. I also observed many positive effects for the children without disabilities in these regular education classrooms.

When we look at a child first as a person, and then take into consideration what adaptations need to be made to accommodate the child's limitation, we are better able to focus on the strengths of the child. For many children with disabilities, sensitivities and strengths develop that can be assets to everyone around them. Children have an innate capacity for caring, encouraging, and accepting a peer, with or without a disability, that we as adults can observe and learn from. For example, I have found that children with limited intelligence can be among the most emotionally warm and caring individuals when interacting with others.

To focus on a child's strengths while taking into account his limitations encourages us as adults to foster and support a child's independence. I first learned this lesson when I was in Junior High School. My mother took care of foster children in our home. Often these children had a disability varying in type and degree of severity. She loved these children and really encouraged each child to stretch to do what she thought the child's capabilities would allow. I observed my mother caring for and working with two pre-school girls who were blind at birth. She carefully instructed them how to do a project and would wait patiently for the girls to attempt to do it. My first inclination was to help them, but my mother always reminded me that they could learn to do it, *and they did.* This was an invaluable lesson for me.

Encouraging independence is a necessary component for a child to gain a sense of competence and self-worth. These qualities, in turn, give a child the confidence he needs to engage in new activities and new learning. With the belief that he has the resources to be successful, a child can approach a task with a positive "I can do it" attitude.

I have found that teaching a child the steps to take to solve problems helps the child develop the skills necessary to find solutions to problems that he encounters in learning and in everyday living. Parents who have used this problem solving process have also found success with it. This process can be taught to children of any age as long as the wording and types of solutions are adapted to the age of the child.

When first teaching this process, your involvement entails guiding the child through the process at least once or twice. As your child develops greater competency with the steps for problem solving, he can do it more on his own until it becomes an automatic process.

The steps to use for problem solving are:

1) <u>Identify the problem</u>.
Children sometimes need help with this, even after they have become very familiar with the process. You can help your child with this step by

talking with him about what he thinks the problem is and then helping him sort out the main issue.

2) <u>Identify the feelings associated with the problem.</u>

This is an important step. The goal is to acknowledge the feelings connected with the problem, put them aside, and then objectively look for a solution to the problem.

3) <u>Brainstorm possible actions to take to resolve the problem.</u>

Brainstorming means first writing down as many ideas as possible without discussing them or making judgments as to whether they will work or not. Initially, include your ideas with the ideas your child provides.

4) <u>Choose one of the actions from the brainstorming list.</u>

For most children, let them choose the action themselves. If your child is hesitant, narrow the choice to three actions and have him choose one of the three.

5) <u>Discuss the probable results of the action</u>.

What can you expect to happen by taking this action to solve the problem?

6) <u>Make a commitment to act on the decision</u>.

Have your child write down the action of his choice and a statement of what he will do to implement his decision.

7) <u>Evaluate the results</u>.

Was the problem resolved? If not, go back to step 3. If your child was successful, congratulate him and encourage him to use this procedure when faced with the next problem. [Form 22 in Appendix A gives you these steps in a format that can be used for recording purposes.]

Communicating with their children on a regular basis is an essential part of every parent's responsibility. As parents and adults, we need to talk *with* children rather than talk *at* them.

In talking and interacting with children over the past several years, I have found them to have understandings and insights about themselves and others that far exceed our expectations. They can come up with ideas and solutions to problems that are creative and "right on" for them. For this to happen, however,

I found I really needed to *listen* to children and *hear* what they were saying, not from *my* perspective as an adult, but from *their* perspective as a child. To do this, I had to put all my judgments, ideas, and expectations aside. For example, when one ten year old was asked if he had anyone at home that he could talk to, he answered, "I can talk to my mom. She listens but she doesn't really hear me because she's always doing the dishes or something else when I talk to her."

We need to *hear* children beyond their words. We need to pay attention to their body language and try to *feel* the emotions behind their words. Often, especially with young children, we get *behaviors* instead of words and have to be creative in order to interpret what they are trying to tell us.

Children with disabilities need to know and understand their strengths and their limitations. This information is best shared with them first by their parents and then by their teachers. These children also need to clearly know that all people can do some things well, yet have difficulty with other things (even adults), and that we all need to work on building our strengths and finding ways to work with our limitations. Children should experience their parents and teachers working together to help them in this process. To do this, I encourage parents to include their children in parent/teacher conferences and when older, in their educational team meeting.

Test scores can be shared with children in a number of ways. This can be done by using a graph such as the one on Form 8. As the child gets older, actual test scores may be shared once the child knows what test scores mean.

The sharing of test results becomes important once children reach about 8 years of age. At this point, they begin comparing themselves to others and it is important for them to know and understand their own uniqueness and individuality as a learner and as a person. Sharing of test results with a child, assuming the test results are valid and the sharing is done in a constructive way, can help a child come to a better understanding of himself as a student. However, there is another caution here. Remember that test results and academic learning are only one aspect of a child; there are also many other mental, emotional, social, spiritual, and physical qualities that define each child.

In most cases, it is best that educators share the test results with a child initially, and then let the child share his understanding of the results with his parents. In this way, parents find out how their child perceives the results of the testing and can help to clear up any misunderstandings about his test scores. If there is a problem, the parent should contact the appropriate teacher and discuss the difficulty. Always remember, when test results are shared and discussed with children, it should be done with discernment.

In our work with children, we need to occasionally stop and reflect on what we are doing to determine if what is being done is in the best interests of the child. It is essential to also determine the effectiveness of what we are doing in helping children feel positive about themselves as people and as learners. Through our reflections, when we see the need for a change, we then need to decide what should be changed, implement the change, and after a period of time, evaluate its effectiveness.

EPILOGUE

There are many new and creative practices that are taking place for children with disabilities in our schools across the United States. The movement toward inclusion is growing, and research is documenting the positive effects of this movement. However, there are several key issues that still must be considered.

Children need to be given a label consistent with the "approved" characteristics of their disability to receive funding for the special services provided by their local school district. In practice, we must go beyond a label in understanding children with disabilities and focus more on the individual child. As mentioned previously, there are overlapping characteristics among children with the same label, but there are more *unique* characteristics for each child than *shared* characteristics. This factor must always be kept in mind as we assess children, decide on program placement, and customize individual educational plans to meet the needs of each child. In designing strategies to meet these needs, we need to focus more on how their strengths can be used to facilitate their learning, as well as teach them ways to cope with their limitations. Within these parameters, we must also retain the perspective of the "whole child."

The number of children being diagnosed and serviced under the categories of Attention Deficit Hyperactivity Disorder, Learning Disability, and Emotional/Behavioral Disorders has increased significantly over the last decade. We need to examine this increase to determine if it is "real" or if some of the increase is due to the lack of a comprehensive evaluation to determine the existence of a disability or disorder, or if it is due to a misdiagnosis. Based on experience, I feel that Attention Deficit Hyperactivity Disorders are being overdiagnosed at this time due to inadequate evaluations. It is imperative that a comprehensive evaluation of a child *precede* the diagnosis of ADHD.

There are many causes for inattentiveness, impulsiveness, and hyper-activity in children. Some of these are linked to what is happening to a child emotionally and situationally. If this is the case, to diagnose a child with ADHD is simply masking the real cause, which prevents the use of the proper corrective actions to effectively treat the problem.

A comprehensive evaluation of ADHD should include:

♦ an interview with the child

♦ an interview with the parent/s

♦ observation of parent-child interactions

♦ classroom observation

♦ parent and teacher behavior rating scales

♦ cognitive evaluations of sustained attention, selective attention, and impulse control

♦ individual ability and achievement testing

Because ADHD has overlapping characteristics with other disorders, if ADHD is indicated (based on this evaluation), one needs to rule out learning dis-abilities, emotional disturbances, and neurological involvement before assigning this diagnosis.

Regarding the increase in other types of disabilities, such as learning disabilities and emotional/behavioral disorders, we need to take some time to evaluate how our schools are currently meeting the needs of children. This is necessary to rule out factors in school practices that may be contributing to this increase in learning and behavioral problems.

In measuring a child's progress, we need to increase our use of more informally gathered information, such as portfolios of the child's work, demon-strations before peers, and other observed applications of knowledge, in addition to the use of standardized tests. This provides a variety of perspectives that indicate the degree to which a child is assimilating his new knowledge. For children who have difficulty demonstrating what they know through the use of tests, this is particularly important.

For all children, and especially children with disabilities, we need to plan and implement curriculum and instructional strategies based on the concept of developmentally appropriate practices. These practices direct us to create materials and expectations that are appropriate for both the age and individual needs of the child. When implemented, these practices provide a sound basis for educating children from the perspective of what is correct for their age, and also for the adaptation of materials and expectations to meet the individual and unique needs of each child. The National Association for the Education of Young Children, the Gesell Institute, and The Society for Developmental Education are organizations currently promoting and training parents and educators in this concept. [See Resources in Appendix A for additional organizations.]

There is a need to go beyond where we have been in education. That is, we need to expand our visions about what education *can* and *should* be for all children. It is essential to do this for children with disabilities. We must learn more about the conditions that affect learning, by researching the presence and extent of various types of stimuli in the environment. We should pay attention to new ways of helping children learn, such as some of the ones listed in the bibliography section of this book.

To make this possible, more collaborative efforts are needed to help bridge the gap between parents and educators that currently occurs in far too many school systems. It takes everyone working together to create, organize, and implement educational practices that will benefit all children.

What we do today for children will be realized in their future. It is our responsibility as parents and educators to create learning environments that will make it possible for *all* children to realize their full potential.

$$\Omega$$

APPENDIX A

FORMS

PARENT SURVEY

1. What are your reactions and feelings to your child's new placement?

2. How does your child feel about the new placement?

3. How is you child coping with the new academic demands of the classroom setting?

4. How would you rate your child's self-esteem in the new setting?

5. How do you feel your child interacts with his/her peers?

6. Have you noticed any changes (positive or negative) in your child since his/her new placement?

7. Can you suggest any ideas or strategies that may assist us in working with your child?

Additional Comments:

© *Peytral Publications*

STUDENT SURVEY

1. How do you feel about you new class placement?

2. How do you feel you are performing in the classroom?

3. Are you following the classroom rules?

4. Are the academic modifications to the curriculum helping you?

5. Are you receiving enough support in the classroom?

6. Are you able to complete the classwork and the home work assignments?

7. How do you get along with the other students in your classroom?

8. Are you involved in extracurricular activities? If the answer is NO, what type of extracurricular activities would you be interested in joining?

© *Peytral Publications*

PARENT'S KNOWLEDGE OF THEIR CHILD

Directions: Answer the questions or statements on this form as completely as possible. Take this form to your child's first educational team meeting with your child's teachers.

1. My child's disability is:_____

2. The date my child was first diagnosed with this disability was:_____

3. My child's disability seems to interfere with learning in the following areas:
    _____
    _____

4. My child's disability affects his feelings about learning in the following ways:
    _____
    _____
    _____

5. Other manifestations of my child's disability include:
    _____
    _____
    _____

6. My child has the following strengths (including strengths both as a person and as a learner):
    _____
    _____
    _____

7. My child's interests and/or hobbies are:
    _____
    _____

8. My child's favorite school subject is : _____

9. My child has expressed the following fears and concerns about learning and school:
    _____
    _____
    _____

© *Peytral Publications*

10. My child seems to learn best under the following conditions or circumstances:

_____

_____

_____

_____

11. I have the following health concerns about my child:

_____

_____

_____

_____

12. Recent family events or changes that may affect my child's learning and/or behavior in school include:

_____

_____

_____

_____

13. Additional information that I would like teachers or other school staff to know about my child:

_____

_____

_____

_____

After you have completed this form, review it and circle the items you particularly want to discuss with your child's educational team.

List here the questions you want to ask at your child's meeting:

_____

_____

_____

_____

List here the information you which to obtain from school staff:

_____

_____

_____

_____

© *Peytral Publications*

SCHOOL MODIFICATIONS

Directions: Have the case manager of your child's educational team complete the following form. This form can then be used by you when helping your child with his homework.

Child's name _____

Grade _____ Date _____

Person completing the form _____

Modifications being used in the school setting. For each type of modification, please indicate both the subject area and the types of modifications being made.

Text book modifications:

_____
_____
_____
_____
_____

Modifications in Daily Assignments:

_____
_____
_____
_____
_____

Modifications in Written Language:

_____
_____
_____
_____
_____

Modifications in Organization of Work Space, Materials and Time:

_____
_____
_____
_____

© *Peytral Publications*

Modifications on Giving Directions:

_____
_____
_____
_____
_____
_____

Modifications for Testing and Assessment:

_____
_____
_____
_____
_____
_____

Other areas such as expectations, behavior, etc. in which modifications are being made for this child at school:

_____
_____
_____
_____
_____

Teachers Observations Regarding this Child's Learning Style:

_____
_____
_____
_____
_____

© *Peytral Publications*

LEARNING DIFFICULTIES CHECKLIST

Directions: Check each behavior you have observed in your child.

❑ Has difficulty following verbal directions.

❑ Has difficulty following written directions.

❑ Does not seem to listen or pay attention.

❑ Gets frustrated easily.

❑ Gives up easily.

❑ Has difficulty following a map or diagram.

❑ Has difficulty remembering instructions and routine tasks.

❑ Has difficulty remembering symbols and words.

❑ Does not follow through with instructions/information.

❑ Takes longer to do some tasks than others.

❑ Often seems to show poor judgment and makes poor decisions

❑ Need concrete examples and demonstrations to understand ideas and concepts

❑ Has trouble relating previously learned information for an extended period of time

❑ Has difficulty memorizing a series of items.

❑ Has difficulty remembering sequences in problem solving.

❑ Has difficulty organizing work space.

❑ Has a poor concept of time.

❑ Does not plan a project in steps.

❑ Does not recognize deadlines for work completion.

❑ Has difficulty working independently.

❑ Is easily distracted from a task.

© *Peytral Publications*

❑ Can tell you the answer but has difficulty writing the answer.

❑ Can respond with, "I know it, but cannot say it".

❑ Can give a quick, brief answer or response but not elaborate.

❑ Is hesitant and shows frustration when responding .

❑ Does not complete his tasks.

❑ Writes illegibly.

❑ Takes excessive time compared to similarly aged peers.

❑ Loses his work.

Note: Checks in the first seven items indicate potential problems in attention, discrimination and/or memory at the input level.

Checks on the second set of fourteen items indicate potential difficulties in processing information.

Checks in the last set of eight items indicate potential difficulties at the output or sharing level.

© *Peytral Publications*

This page left blank to ensure proper forms flow

ATTENTION DIFFICULTIES CHECKLIST
(BEHAVIORS ASSOCIATED WITH ADHD)

Directions: Check each behavior you have observed in your child.

❑ Being always "on the go" or often acting as if "driven by a motor."

❑ Often fidgets with hands or feet.

❑ Often has difficulty playing or engaging in leisure activities alone.

❑ Often talks excessively.

❑ Often runs about or climbs inappropriately (in adolescents or adults, this may be limited to restlessness).

❑ Often has difficulty awaiting his turn.

❑ Often interrupts or intrudes on others.

❑ Often dislikes or avoids engaging in tasks that require sustained mental effort (such as homework).

❑ Is often distracted by what is happening around him.

❑ Has difficulty organizing things and activities.

❑ Often does not complete tasks or chores.

❑ Often misses details or makes careless mistakes while doing something.

This information should be shared with your child's educational team and teachers to determine if these same behaviors are seen in the school setting and how frequently.

© *Peytral Publications*

A CHILD'S VIEW OF WHAT LEARNING IS LIKE

Directions: Have your child respond to each question as completely as possible. For younger children and children who have difficulty writing, read the question to your child and write his response for him.

1. What do you like about reading?

   _____
   _____
   _____
   _____

2. What do you find the most difficult for you when reading?

   _____
   _____
   _____
   _____
   _____

3. What do you enjoy about working with numbers?

   _____
   _____
   _____
   _____

4. What parts of math do you find easy?/difficult?

   _____
   _____
   _____
   _____

5. Do you enjoy writing? Why?

   _____
   _____
   _____
   _____

© *Peytral Publications*

6. Is it easier to tell someone the answer to a question or to write down your answer? What makes it easier?/harder?

_____
_____
_____
_____

7. Do you like to write stories? Why?

_____
_____
_____
_____

8. Do you like to write reports? Why?

_____
_____
_____
_____

9. Add any other questions you would find useful

_____
_____
_____
_____

© *Peytral Publications*

HOW I SEE MYSELF COMPARED TO OTHERS

Directions: Have your child put an "x" to show how he is doing in reading, math, written work, etc., compared to other kids at the same grade level. Rather than using exact numerical scores with your child, use phrases such as "like most other kids" for placement with the average range, "not as well as other kids" for below average and "better than other kids" for above average. If your child understands the term "average," you can use the terminology on the graph.

GRAPHING HOW I SEE MYSELF

Above Average _____

Average _____ 68 % of all students

Below Average _____

Once your child has completed the graph, use the following statements and questions to gain additional information about your child. This information can be used for setting goals and charting your child's academic progress.

1. Tell me about your best subjects:

    _____

    _____

    _____

    _____

© *Peytral Publications*

Form 8 (cont.)

2. Tell me about the subjects in which you feel you are not doing as well as the other kids.

3. What changes would you like to make in any of these subjects?

4. What ideas do you have for making these changes?

5. How can I help you to be successful in making these changes?

6. What ideas do you have as to how your teachers can help you?

7. Do you have any other thoughts about your learning?

© Peytral Publications

This page left blank to ensure proper forms flow

PARENT OBSERVATION OF WORK HABITS

Directions: Record observations of your child's work habits by checking next to YES or NO after each of the statements or questions listed below. You may choose to use a different form for each subject area.

Subject Area _____ Date _____

❑YES ❑NO   My child shows a positive attitude toward this subject.

❑YES ❑NO   My child shows a negative attitude toward this subject.

❑YES ❑NO   My child shows a neutral attitude toward this subject.

❑YES ❑NO   My child has his materials ready and organized for working on this subject.

❑YES ❑NO   My child knows how to get started on his assignment.

❑YES ❑NO   My child understands what he needs to do to complete the work for this subject.

❑YES ❑NO   My child sustains attention while working on this subject.

❑YES ❑NO   My child frequently asks me for help.

❑YES ❑NO   My child appears to have the skills necessary to successfully complete the work.

❑YES ❑NO   My child takes an excessive amount of time to complete the work for this subject.

❑YES ❑NO   My child gives up easily or "shuts down" before the work is completed.

❑YES ❑NO   My child puts down any answer just to get the work finished.

These observations can be used to determine which of your child's work habits help and which ones interfere with his success. Goals can then be developed to help your child make changes in the work habits that limit his success.

© *Peytral Publications*

INFORMATION PROCESSING

Directions: Check each behavior you have observed in your child.

My child seems to react to events and organizes materials and activities in these ways:

- ❑ Likes routine in his environment.
- ❑ Likes order in his environment.
- ❑ Likes rules to follow when doing something.
- ❑ Likes to know exactly what is expected of him.
- ❑ Notices and tunes into details.
- ❑ Recalls details well.
- ❑ Responds well to verbal explanations.
- ❑ Is good at memorizing facts.
- ❑ Likes consistency from day to day.
- ❑ For any new experience, wants to know in advance what will take place.
- ❑ Wants facts.
- ❑ Likes to work in a step-by-step order in doing things.
- ❑ Uses a logical approach to problem solving.
- ❑ Likes to verbalize his experience.
- ❑ Likes to learn from books.

- ❑ Likes change.
- ❑ Likes flexibility in what he does.
- ❑ Likes choices.
- ❑ Sees and understands the "big picture" of an event/story.
- ❑ Forgets facts and details.
- ❑ Likes to work with pictures.
- ❑ Likes and understands visual patterns.
- ❑ Has difficulty organizing his time.
- ❑ Has difficulty organizing materials.
- ❑ Likes to link current events to past events.
- ❑ Likes being involved with people.
- ❑ Likes music and movement.
- ❑ Works best when he can move around.
- ❑ Does more than one thing at a time.
- ❑ May do things for the fun of doing them rather than the outcome.
- ❑ Does not see the importance of time.
- ❑ Likes doing models.

See instructions on next page

© *Peytral Publications*

To use this information, count the number of checks in each of the two sets of behaviors divided by the dotted line. If your child has a predominant number of checks in the top set, he may be more of a sequential learner than a simultaneous (random) learner. If there are many more checks in the bottom set of behaviors, your child is most likely more of a simultaneous or random learner than he is a sequential learner. If there are about an equal number of checks in each set, your child is most likely and integrated learner. That is, he can react, respond, and organize events in his world both ways and is equally proficient in both. This information can be further verified by your child's teachers.

Information about your child's learning style can be used to gain a better understanding of how your child experiences and structures his world. This information should also be taken into account in planning learning strategies and learning environments that will support a greater degree of success in learning for your child.

© *Peytral Publications*

LEARNING STYLE CHECKLIST
(For children 10 and older)

Directions: Have your child check the behaviors that describe him.

A. I see myself as someone who:

- ❑ likes to be with people
- ❑ is sensitive to how others feel
- ❑ is creative
- ❑ likes to learn things that are meaningful to me
- ❑ likes to collect things and save them
- ❑ likes to have a lot of information about something at one time
- ❑ likes to work on my own time schedule
- ❑ makes decisions because they "feel" right
- ❑ enjoys learning in a group
- ❑ is concerned about fairness
- ❑ needs time balanced between play and work
- ❑ does not like conflict or disagreements
- ❑ likes to have time to think about things

_____TOTAL

B. I see myself as someone who:

- ❑ likes to work with ideas and thoughts
- ❑ likes my work to be organized and neat
- ❑ prefers to work alone
- ❑ likes to have enough time to learn something thoroughly
- ❑ likes to debate or argue about ideas
- ❑ likes finding answers
- ❑ likes books
- ❑ likes things to be predictable
- ❑ likes to have things right
- ❑ judges the value or importance of something
- ❑ takes learning seriously
- ❑ is good at integrating information to form a new idea
- ❑ likes a quiet environment in which to work

_____TOTAL

© *Peytral Publications*

C. *I see myself as someone who:*

- ❑ learns best through practical, hands-on ways
- ❑ likes to have rules to follow
- ❑ likes everything to be in its place and organized
- ❑ likes to work one step at a time
- ❑ wants to know what is expected of me
- ❑ likes to have a specific time for doing things
- ❑ likes to have a finished product for my efforts
- ❑ likes to work with details
- ❑ likes approval for my work
- ❑ likes to have a consistent way of doing things
- ❑ wants to create practical products
- ❑ likes things to be accurate and precise
- ❑ thinks about what I'm going to do before I do it

_____ TOTAL

D. *I see myself as someone who:*

- ❑ likes change
- ❑ sees the world as a laboratory to explore
- ❑ is very curious
- ❑ thrives on new experiences
- ❑ likes to be "on the go"
- ❑ likes to do several things at one time
- ❑ likes choices
- ❑ likes to do things on my own
- ❑ gets more involved in the process of doing than on the outcome
- ❑ is independent
- ❑ is flexible in how I do things
- ❑ likes to do the unusual
- ❑ gets so involved with what I am doing that I forget about time
- ❑ prefers to construct a model by looking at its picture rather than by reading the directions

_____ TOTAL

See instructions on next page

© *Peytral Publications*

This form has been divided into 4 sections, labeled A, B, C, and D, which will help you determine the most comfortable learning style of your child. If the totals are similar in each of the sections, your child is most likely an integrated learner who shows no particular preference in his learning style. If he has a majority of checks in category A, he shares characteristics with people who have an abstract random style of learning. Category B lists characteristics for abstract sequential learners, category C, concrete sequential learners, and category D, concrete random learners. A more complex learning style inventory should be taken for further verification.

© *Peytral Publications*

This page left blank to ensure proper forms flow

Form 12

ABILITY, ACHIEVEMENT, AND PERFORMANCE RELATIVE TO LEARNING

Eligibility for Special Education Services for children with learning disabilities is based on the results of standardized test scores in addition to performance on school assignments. Standardized test scores include a child's score on an *ability* test (such as the Wechsler Intelligence Scale for Children) and a child's reading, math, and written language scores on an *achievement* test (such as the Woodcock Johnson Tests of Achievement).

To meet the criteria for special education placement, a child must have a *severe* discrepancy between his *ability* and *achievement* test scores and be performing at a level that is significantly below the expectation for his measured ability. What constitutes a severe discrepancy is generally defined by the Special Education section of the various state Departments of Education. The guidelines or mandates defined by each state's Department of Education are then implemented by the individual school districts within each state. The criteria for determining eligibility of a child for special education services can best be obtained from the child's school district.

The most common terms used in this assessment process are defined below:

Cognitive Ability or Intelligence: one's capacity to learn; one's proficiency in solving problems.

Achievement: what one has learned; skills one has acquired through teaching and/or experience.

Performance: how one does on assignments or tasks.

EXAMPLE: Jerry, a fourth grader, had the following scores documented on his Individual Educational Plan.

His *cognitive ability* was a standard score of 109 +/- 5
(=73%, upper limits of the average range).

His *achievement* scores were:
reading:	a standard score of 83 (+/- 4) (=13%, below average range).
math:	a standard score of 108 (+/- 4) (=70%, upper limits of the average range).
written language:	a standard score of 90 (+/- 4) (=25%, lower limits of the average range).

© *Peytral Publications*

To determine if a severe discrepancy exists between Jerry's *ability* and *achievement* scores, one needs to compare each of the three subject areas to his score on the WISC-III. This can be accomplished by comparing the scores directly to the formula used by the school district. This comparison is plotted on the graph that follows.

DISCREPANCIES OF ABILITY/ACHIEVEMENT/PERFORMANCE

SS	Math				Written Language				Reading			%
	Ab	Ach	P		Ab	Ach	P		Ab	Ach	P	
125												95%
120												91%
115												84%
110	▓	▓	▓		▓				▓			75%
105	▓	▓	▓		▓				▓			63%
100	▓				▓				▓			50%
95												37%
90						▓	▓					25%
85						▓	▓			▓		16%
80										▓	▓	9%
75										▓		5%

SS: Standard Scores	**%**: Percentile Scores
Ab: Cognitive Ability	**Ach**: Achievement
P: Performance (estimated by your child's teachers)	

According to the point difference between Jerry's *ability* and *achievement* scores in each of the three subject areas, one can see that no discrepancy exists between Jerry's *ability* score and his *achievement* score in math. His *performance* in this area also indicates he is doing well on his math assignments.

Jerry's *achievement* score and *performance* in written language is somewhat lower than his *ability* score but would probably not be considered severe enough to warrant the need for special education services. This example should be used for understanding only; it is not meant as criteria for eligibility.

In reading, Jerry scored significantly below the expectation for his *ability*. Generally, this degree of difference is considered a *severe* discrepancy. If Jerry is not making progress consistent with his *ability* due to *processing difficulties*, then he would be eligible to receive special services in the area of reading. This need if further supported because his daily *performance* in reading is also significantly lower than one would expect given average *ability*.

© *Peytral Publications*

Form 13

AN APPRAISAL OF YOUR CHILD'S SCHOOL PERFORMANCE

Name_____	How I am Doing in School Date Completed_____					
	Reading Yes / No	Math Yes / No	Writing Yes / No	Art Yes / No	Science Yes / No	etc.
I am doing satisfactory work						
I complete all my assignments						
I like this subject						
(Add more as needed)						

Directions:

1) Put aside time to meet with your child to discuss the purpose of the chart and to get information from him.

2) List the subject areas your child is currently taking across the top of the chart. Have your child do the writing (or you do it if your child prefers) in the order in which the child thinks of them. You may add other areas of school life, such as friends, if you wish.

3) Have your child answer each question for each area by putting a check in either the **Yes** or **No** column.

4) Highlight all the **Yes**'s in each column with a colored (i.e., green) highlight pen.

5) Circle the **No**'s in pencil for each column.

6) Use your child's most recent report card and information from your child's teachers to verify your child's perceptions about how he is doing. If any of these are inaccurate, discuss the reasons why with your child and change the response on the chart.

© *Peytral Publications*

1) Make a list of the **No**'s for each area on a separate sheet of paper.

2) Make a decision as to which **No**'s are the most important to work on first. It is best to start out with no more than 2 or 3 areas and put the others on hold for a later time.

3) Circle the items chosen to be worked on. Have your child write a goal for each item relative to what he needs to do to move this item to the **Yes** column on this chart.

4) For ease in charting, record the items and goals on a new form, such as Form 14 on the next page in this Appendix.

© *Peytral Publications*

Form 14
<u>CHARTING MY PROGRESS</u>

AREAS TO BE WORKED ON														
Name						Month								
Area	Goal	Week 1			Week 2			Week 3			Week 4			
		Y	P	N	Y	P	N	Y	P	N	Y	P	N	

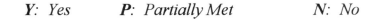

Y: Yes   *P: Partially Met*   *N: No*

Directions:

1). Check your child's progress at the end of each week. If your child has achieved his goal, have him put a check in the Yes column. If he partially met his goal (i.e., 3 of the 5 days that week), put 3/5 in the P (partially met) column. If your child made no progress toward his goal, discuss ways to change his approach so he can make progress the next week.

2). As each goal is achieved, go back to the "How I Am Doing" Chart (Form 13), and have your child erase the appropriate No check, put a check in the Yes column and highlight it with green.

3). Repeat this process until all the **NO** checks have been erased and all checks are in the **YES** column highlighted by a green marker. It is important to praise your child on completion of each goal. When the chart is all green (or mostly green), have a special celebration with your child.

4). Each time your child receives his report card, start again with #1, revising and updating the information on your child's school performance as needed.

Note: You may want to put these charts in a special folder so you and your child can refer to them at the end of the current school year and save them for future reference.

© *Peytral Publications*

CHARTING STANDARDIZED TEST SCORES

Directions: Obtain your child's standardized test scores from his Individual Education Plan (Assessment Section) or from you child's Case Manager. Plot your child's scores on the graph provided below. If quantitative scores are not available, use the general categories of Average (90 - 109), Below Average (= to or < 84), or Above Average (= to or > than 110).

SS >								%>
135								
130								98%
125								
120								
115								84%
110								
105								
100								50%
95								
90								
85								16%
80								
75								
70								2%
<								<
	Reading	**Math**	**Writing**	**Science**	**Sec. Std**	**etc.**	**etc.**	

SS: Standard Scores   **<**: Less than
%: Percentile Scores   **>**: More than

Each subsequent time your child is tested, record his scores on this graph. For each set of test scores, record the date the test was taken. Record each set in a different color or use different types of lines in the plotting of the scores. You can then use this graphic representation of your child's test scores to measure your child's academic progress as portrayed by standardized test scores. In doing this, it is important to remember this is only one picture of your child's progress.

© *Peytral Publications*

HOMEWORK MATERIALS

Basic Materials Needed:

✓ Paper - including pads of paper, notebook paper, and paper without lines. Lined paper should vary in line size according to the age of the child. If a child has small motor difficulties, larger spaced lined paper is often best.

✓ Pencils - preferably #2 hardness.

✓ Crayons - colored pencils for older children

✓ Pens - have 3 or 4 different colors available

✓ Eraser

✓ Ruler - purchase one with larger numbers for younger children

✓ Folders of various colors

✓ Assignment Notebook

✓ Scissors

✓ Note pads of varying sizes

Optional Materials:

✓ Chips for sorting and counting

✓ Number line and/or Alphabet line

✓ Matrix for multiplication facts

✓ Calculator

✓ Protractor

✓ Pencil grip holder

✓ Dictionary

© *Peytral Publications*

HOMEWORK SCHEDULE

Name _____ Week of _____

Directions: Block in the times available for homework. Designate one or two days of the week as free days. This can vary every week.

	MON.	TUES.	WED	THURS.	FRI.	SAT	SUN
Morning							
Afternoon							
Evening							

Assignments to be Completed

Directions: Have your child list the specific homework to be completed for each day. The work should be listed and prioritized. Have your child estimate the time needed for each assignment. Mark when it is completed and go on to the next assignment.

Date _____ Day of the Week_____

What Needs to be Done	Approximate Time Needed	Completed

Note: You may wish to laminate this Form rather than duplicate it.

© *Peytral Publications*

This page left blank to ensure proper forms flow

LEARNING ENVIRONMENT NEEDS

Work Space

Degree of quietness needed: _____

Amount of distraction tolerable: _____

These people may have access to my child's designated work space:

_____

Organization of Materials

Degree of organization needed for materials: _____

Additional materials or aids my child needs for successful completion of assignments: _____

_____

Work Time

My child can be expected to do homework up to: _____minutes and/or hours per day.

The longest period of time my child can work before taking a break is: _____

My child should prioritize his assignments from difficult to medium to easy and then decide which one he would prefer to start with:_____

_____

Other Considerations

_____

_____

Note: These decisions should be changed and adjusted depending upon your child's success in completing his homework.

© *Peytral Publications*

Form 19

DETERMINING OPTIMUM ENVIRONMENTS FOR EACH LEARNING STYLE

Directions: Based on the information gathered from Forms 10 and 11, or other documentation you have, check each strategy below that specifically fits your child. It is best if you and your child fill out this form together. You may also want to consult your child's teachers for their input.

Sequential learners, concrete sequential learners, abstract sequential learners, and verbal learners learn best when they have:

❑ a quiet, predictable work environment

❑ materials and study area organized neatly

❑ time lines to follow that are clearly stated

❑ an understanding of what to do and how to do it

❑ procedures for learning organized in a step-by-step manner

❑ assignments in which they think and problem solve in words

❑ consistency and structure in their learning environment

❑ consistency in expectations

❑ everything clearly defined by rules

❑ a goal to work toward

❑ a situation in which they can work alone

❑ a reward system and/or approval for the work they do

Simultaneous learners, concrete random learners, abstract random learners and visual learners learn best when they have:

❑ an environment that allows for flexibility and choice

❑ materials accessible, but having a choice for organizing:

© *Peytral Publications*

Form 19 (cont.)

- ❏ by color, shape, function, etc.
- ❏ blocks of time in which to work where there are built-in breaks
- ❏ the "big picture" of what they are to do
- ❏ several pieces of information available to them at one time
- ❏ encouragement to make mental pictures of verbal information
- ❏ the opportunity to use pictures, charts, maps and other visual aids to use in thinking and problem solving
- ❏ a chance to make choices from two or more options
- ❏ flexibility in how they arrive at an answer or an outcome
- ❏ the opportunity to share what they are doing with another person
- ❏ the opportunity to work with others

Note: This information can be integrated with the information on Form 18 and incorporated into a list of strategies that help your child to be more efficient when doing homework assignments and more successful in learning.

© Peytral Publications

MIND MAPPING

To create a mind map:

1) Start with an **object** word (such as *dog, house,* etc.) for younger children. For older children, start with a **concept** word (a word we use to mean some kind of idea or event, such as *animal, learning, parade, picnic, fireworks,* etc.

2) Have your child make a mental picture of the object or concept word in his head. Then you or your child *write down* all the words that come to mind when describing the chosen word or

3) *Make a list* of words that come to mind when you hear the object or concept word.

4) Put the object or concept word either in the center or on the top of the space you will be working on. Use **linking** words (*is, are, have,* etc.) to connect each word to the main word.

5) Have your child keep adding new words that come to mind until he has reached a sense of completion. You may use either linking words with the connecting lines or connecting lines only.

6) On completion, have your child verbalize the information generated by the mind map.

7) Have your child use the information from the mind map to either create a picture to convey the information or to put the information into narrative form.

© *Peytral Publications*

Mind Mapping using **Object** Words:

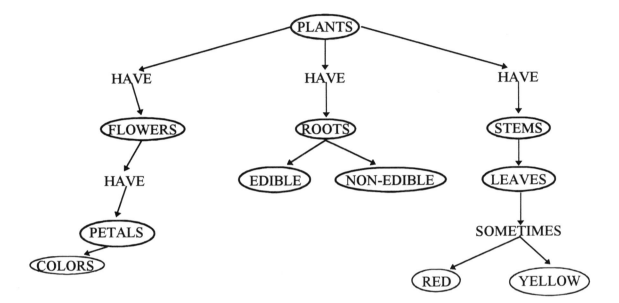

© *Peytral Publications*

Mind Mapping using **Concept** Words:

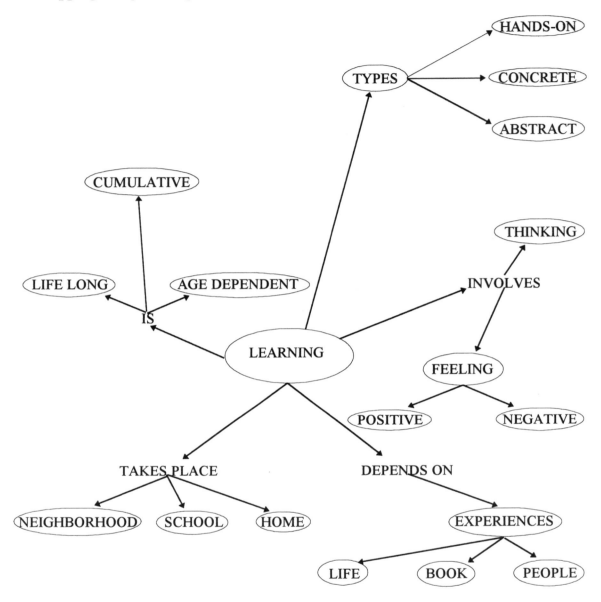

Remember: Mind mapping can act as a springboard for generating and creating limitless ideas. Have fun with the process and join in with your child when it is appropriate.

© *Peytral Publications*

Form 21

SUPPORTIVE WORDS AND PHRASES

1. You did very well
2. Good for you!
3. You're on the right track
4. You're really improving
5. I knew you could do it
6. Good work
7. Awesome
8. Terrific!
9. Superb
10. Marvelous!
11. You're doing great
12. Outstanding!
13. That's coming along nicely.
14. You figured that out fast.
15. I'm proud of the way you worked today!
16. Tremendous!
17. You certainly did well today.
18. Perfect!
19. Nice going.
20. WOW!
21. Wonderful!
22. You're learning more every day.
23. Super!
24. You did a lot of work today!
25. Congratulations
26. Excellent!
27. Sensational!
28. You're doing beautifully
29. Way to go!
30. Good thinking
31. Fantastic!
32. Right on!
33. Great!
34. I knew you could do it!
35. Good job.
36. Good memory.
37. You really make this fun
38. It's coming.
39. You're almost there.
40. Let's celebrate!
41. You're doing just fine
42. You've figured it out!
43. Keep it up!
44. It's getting better.
45. Your work looks great!
46. That's quality work!
47. Dynamite!
48. Great accomplishment!

© *Peytral Publications*

STEPS FOR PROBLEM SOLVING

1. State the nature of the problem.

2. Identify the feelings associated with the problem.

3. Brainstorm possible actions to take to resolve the problem.

4. Choose one of the actions.

5. Discuss the probable results of the action.

6. Make a commitment to act on the decision. Put it in writing.

7. Evaluate the results. If the problem is resolved, celebrate. If not, go back to step 3.

© *Peytral Publications*

APPENDIX B - BIBLIOGRAPHY

Alexander-Roberts, Colleen. *The ADHD Parenting Handbook.* Dallas, TX: Taylor Publishing Co., 1994

Alexander-Roberts, Colleen. *A Parent's Guide to Making it Through the Tough Years: ADHD and Teens.* Dallas, TX: Taylor Publishing Co., 1995.

Anderson, E., Redman, G., & Rogers, C. *Self-Esteem for Tots to Teens.* Wayzata, MN: Parenting & Teaching Publications, 1991.

Armstrong, Thomas, Ph.D. *In Their Own Way: Discovering and Encouraging Your Child's Personal Learning Style.* New York, NY: G.P. Putnam's Sons, 1987.

Bailey, Sally. *Wings to Fly: Bringing Theater Arts to Students with Special Needs.* Rockville, MD: Woodbine House, 1993.
[Chapter 2].

Bain, Lisa J. *A Parent's Guide to Attention Deficit Disorders.* New York, NY: Dell Publishing, 1991. [Chapter 10 - Nontraditional Therapies].

Clarke, Jean Illslely. *Self-Esteem: A Family Affair.* Minneapolis, MN: Winston Press, 1978.

Conners, C. Keith. *Feeding the Brain: How Foods Affect Children.* New York, NY: Plenum, 1989.

Crook, William G., MD. *Help for the Hyperactive Child: A Good-sense Guide for Parents of Children with Hyperactivity, Attention Deficits, and Other Behavior and Learning Problems.* Jackson, TN: Professional Books, Inc., 1991.

Faber, Adele & Mazlish, Elaine. *How to Talk So Kids Can Learn at Home and in School.* New York, NY: Rawson Associates, 1995.

Fisher, Gary, Ph.D. & Cummings, Rhoda, Ed.D. *The Survival Guide for Kids with L.D.* Minneapolis, MN: Free Spirit Publishing, Inc., 1990.

Fisher, Gary, Ph.D. & Cummings, Rhoda, Ed.D. *When Your Child Has L.D.* Minneapolis, MN: Free Spirit Publishing, Inc., 1995.

Garber, Stephen W., Garber, Marianne Daniels, & Spizman, Robyn. *Is Your Child Hyperactive? Inattentive? Impulsive? Distractible? Helping the ADD/Hyperactive Child.* New York, NY: Villard Books, 1995.

Gardner, Howard. *Frames of the Mind: The Theory of Multiple Intelligences.* New York, NY: Basic Books, Inc., 1985

Getskow, Veronica & Konczal, Dee. *Kids with Special Needs: Information and Activities to Promote Awareness and Understanding.* Santa Barbara, CA: The Learning Works, Inc., 1996.

Hammeken, Peggy. *Inclusion: 450 Strategies for Success.* Minnetonka, MN: Peytral Publications, 1995.

Kagan, Jerome. *The Nature of the Child.* New York, NY: Basic Books, 1995.

Kline, Peter. *The Everyday Genius: Restoring Children's Natural Joy of Learning - And Yours, Too.* Arlington, VA: Great Ocean Publishers, 1988.

Kravets, Marybeth & Wax,Imy F., editors. *The K & W Guide to Colleges for the Learning Disabled, Third Edition.* Cambridge, MA: Educators Publishing Service, Inc., 1995.

Levine, Dr. Mel, *All Kinds of Minds: A Young Student's Book About Learning Abilities and Learning Disorders.* Cambridge, MA: Educators Publishing Service, Inc., 1993.

Levine, Dr. Mel, *Educational Care: A System for Understanding and Helping Children with Learning Problems at Home and in School.* Cambridge, MA: Educators Publishing Service, Inc., 1994.

Levine, Dr. Mel. *Keeping Ahead in School: A Student's Book About Learning Abilities and Learning Disorders.* Cambridge, MA: Educators Publishing Service, Inc., 1990.

Mangrum II, Charles T. & Strichart, Stephen S., editors. *Peterson's Colleges with Programs for Students with Learning Disabilities, Fourth Edition.* Princeton, NJ: Peterson's Guides, 1994.

McGee-Cooper, Ann. *Time Management for Unmanageable People.* Dallas, TX: Ann McGee-Cooper & Associates, 1983.

Ostrander, Sheila & Schroeder, Lynn, with Ostrander, Nancy. *Super-Learning 2000.* New York, NY: Delacorte Press, 1994.
[See Chapter 31: Breakthroughs for the Learning Disabled.]

Parents' Educational Resource Center. *For the High School Student: Improving Reading, Taking Tests, and Planning for the Future.* 1660 South Amphlett Blvd., Suite 200, San Mateo, CA: The Parents' Educational Resource Center, 1995.

Redman, George. *Building Self-Esteem in Children: A Skill and Strategy Workbook for Parents.* Wayzata, MN: Parenting and Teaching Publications, 1991.

Rosemond, John. *Ending the Homework Hassles: How to Help Your Child Succeed Independently in School.* Fairway, KS: Andrews, McMeel & Parker, 1990.

Rosemond, John. *Six Point Plan for Raising Happy, Healthy Children.* Kansas City, MO: Andrews & McMeel, 1989.

Samples, Bob. *Open Mind, Whole Mind: Parenting and Teaching Tomorrow's Children Today.* Rollings Hills Estates, CA: Jalmar Press, 1987.

Vitale, Barbara Meister. *Unicorns Are Real.* Rolling Hills Estates, CA: Jalmar Press, 1982.

Vitale, Barbara Meister. *Free Flight: Celebrating Your Right Brain.* Rolling Hills Estates, CA: Jalmar Press, 1986.

Wycoff, Joyce. *Mindmapping: Your Personal Guide to Exploring Creativity and Problem-Solving.* New York, NY: The Berkley Publishing Group, 1991.

Misc. Publications:

Moore, Lorraine, Ph.D. *Learning: What It Is and How Parents Can Help.* Ft. Collins, CO: Raine Publications, 1986.
[available from the author].

Learning Styles: A Guide For Parents. Center for the Study of Learning and Teaching Styles, St. John's University, Grand Central and Utopia Parkways, New York, NY 11439.

What Every Parent Should Know About Reading Disorders. Channing L. Bete Company, Inc., 200 State Road, South Deerfield, MA, 01373.

What Every Parent Should Know About Learning Disabilities. Channing L. Bete Company, Inc., 200 State Road, South Deerfield, MA, 01373

APPENDIX C - RESOURCES

National Organizations:
American Speech-Language Hearing Association
10801 Rockville Peak
Rockville, MD. 20852
800-638-8255

Autism Society of America
8601 Georgia Avenue, Suite 503
Silver Spring, MD. 20901
301-565-0433

Beach Center on Families and Disability
c/o Institute for Life Span Studies
The University of Kansas
3111 Haworth Hall
Lawrence, KS 66045
913-864-7600
[general information on disabilities]

Children with Attention Deficit Disorder
(CHADD)
499 NW 70th Avenue, Suite 109
Plantation, FL. 33317
305-587-3700

Coordinating Council for Handicapped Children
20 East Jackson Blvd., Room 900
Chicago, IL 60604
312-939-3513

Council for Exceptional Children (CEC)
1920 Association Drive
Reston, VA. 22091
703-620-3660
[a resource for all exceptional children]

Feingold Association of the United States (Diet)
P.O. Box 6550
Alexander, VA. 22306
703-768-FAUS

Learning Disabilities Association of America
(LDA)
4156 Library Road
Pittsburgh, PA 15234
412-341-1515

National Association of the Deaf
814 Thayer Avenue
Silver Springs, MD 20910

National Association on Mental Retardation
500 East Border Street, Suite #300
Arlington, TX 76010
817-261-6003

National Association for Visually Handicapped
305 East 24th St., #17C
New York, NY 10010

National Center for Learning Disabilities (NCLD)
381 Park Avenue South, Suite 1420
New York, NY 10016
212-545-7510

National Down Syndrome Congress
1605 Chantilly Road
Atlanta, GA. 30324
800-232-NDSC

National Easter Seal Society
70 East Lake St.
Chicago, IL 60601
800-211-6827

National Information Center for Children and
Youth with Disabilities (NICHCY)
PO Box 1492
Washington, DC 20013
703-893-6061

National Information Center for Handicapped
Children and Youth
1555 Wilson Blvd.
Rosslyn, VA 22209
[source of general information on handicaps)

National Information Center on Deafness
800 Florida Avenue NE
Washington, DC 20022-3695
202-651-5051

National Organization on Disability
910 - 16th St. NW, Suite 200
Washington, DC 20036
800-248-ABCE

Self-Help for Hard of Hearing People
7800 Wisconsin Avenue
Bethesda, MD 20814
301-657-2248

United Cerebral Palsy Association
1522 K Street NW, Suite 1112
Washington, DC 20036
800-872-5UCP

[Contact these national organizations for
information on state and local chapters.]

APPENDIX D - GLOSSARY

The words contained in this glossary are defined in the context in which they are found in this book. They are not meant to be complete definitions.

abstract thinking - that which involves the realm of ideas, thoughts, and symbols (the non-physical).

achievement - an accomplishment in learning or in the completion of a project.

ADD - see Attention Deficit Disorder

ADHD - see Attention Deficit Hyperactivity Disorder

age equivalent score - based on the average performance of children at a particular age level; expressed as a numerical value, first by year and then by month of a child's age.

attention - the ability to focus and remain focused on the task at hand.

auditory memory - that which is used to remember and recall verbal information.

auditory processing - the understanding and use of verbal information.

associative functions - the linking of similar types of information; those which bridge ideas or experiences, or ideas with experiences.

attention deficit disorder - a condition in which a child has difficulties in directing and maintaining attention to tasks. This behavior is significantly different from the behaviors of similarly aged peers.

attention deficit hyperactivity disorder - a condition in which a child has significant difficulties in focusing and sustaining attention, impulsiveness, and regulating his activity level.

collaboration - a team effort based on the idea of working together effectively and providing mutual emotional, mental, or physical support for one another.

cognitive ability - intelligence; one's proficiency in problem solving; one's capacity to learn.

disability - impairment of normal functioning.

discrimination - ability to differentiate between visual, auditory, tactual, or other sensory stimuli.

distractibility/distraction - the result of being easily influenced by external stimuli (such as visible objects and sound) that takes one's focus away from the task at hand.

small motor development (fine motor) - use of small muscle groups for specific tasks such as handwriting.

grade equivalent score - based on the performance of typical students at each grade level. This score is expressed as a numerical grade level and month of that grade level ranging from September (month 1) to June (month 9).

hyperactivity - excessive activity in relation to others of the same age and in similar situations, often expressed as non-stop body movements or excessive verbalization.

IEP - see Individualized Education Plan.

impulsivity/impulsiveness - reacting or responding quickly, without thinking.

inclusive schooling - the practice of educating children with and without disabilities together in the same classroom setting.

individual education plan (IEP)- a written plan for the educational program of a child with disabilities. This plan is developed by the local school in accordance with rules adopted by the state and in accordance with the Individuals with Disabilities Act. An IEP is written for a 12 month period and must be reviewed and revised annually.

information processing - the mental manipulation of words, symbols, and perceptions necessary to acquire knowledge and solve problems.

integrative function - the process of combining one or more functions together, such as the integration of visual and auditory functions, eye and motor functions, etc.

learning disability - a condition in which a child is achieving and performing at a level in reading, math, and/or written language that is significantly below the expectation for his measured intellectual ability. This discrepancy must be due to difficulties in information processing rather than for environmental or other reasons.

learning style - refers to the way a person organizes and responds to experiences and information.

least restrictive environment - an environment for children with disabilities which, to the greatest degree possible, approximates the learning conditions and learning environment of regular education students.

memory - the psychological process involved with remembering visual, auditory, and/or tactile stimuli.

> **immediate memory** - involves the taking in of information and instantaneously repeating it back.

> **short-term memory** - involves the holding of information in one's memory bank for at least 30 seconds and then either repeating it back in the same form using it to solve problems or storing it in long-term memory; working memory.

> **long-term memory** - storing information in one's memory bank for future use; the length of time may vary from several minutes to an indefinite period of time.

modifications - adaptations made in the curriculum, presentation method, or the environment to provide support for the individual child.

mental image - the picture created in one's head of words, symbols, or pictures.

mnemonics - a technique to help one remember and retrieve information. It is the process of creating rhymes, stories, acronyms, pictures, etc. to help your memory retain and recall information.

motor development - involves the growth of large and small muscles in the body needed to perform tasks involving movement of the various body parts, eye movements and eye/hand coordination .

percentile score - a standard score that tells how a child scored compared to other children. This score tells how many children (expressed as a percentile) scored above and below a particular child.

periodic review - a review of a child's individual educational plan that is required by law to occur minimally on an annual basis.

psychological processes - mental functions involved with taking in information, organizing it, transforming it, storing it, and using it.

regular education classroom - a classroom for all children within a school setting.

resource room - a place designated as a classroom for students to go to in order to receive special education services.

sequential processing - taking in, organizing, and responding to information in a step-by-step, linear way where the order of the facts (information) is important in arriving at a solution.

simultaneous processing - taking in, organizing, and responding to information all at once; seeing and relating to the "big picture" where the information is randomly ordered.

standard deviation - a commonly used measure of the extent to which scores deviate from the mean (average).

standard score - a raw score (based on the number correct) that has been transformed to have a given mean (mid-point) and standard deviation from the mean. A common number used to denote the mid-point of the average range is 100 with a standard deviation of 15 points. Any test that has 100 at the mid-point and a standard deviation of 15 can be compared to one another.

standardized scores - raw scores that have been transformed to have a given mean and standard deviation based on a defined population used in the standardization sample.

strategies - techniques or tools to help one approach learning and problem solving in a systematic way.

team teaching - two teachers working together jointly to develop, plan and teach a lesson.

verbal abilities - the understanding, manipulation, and expression of information and ideas in words.

visual/spatial abilities - the understanding and manipulation of material presented through pictures, symbols, and models, and responding to their spatial placement.

visual processing - the understanding and use of information presented in pictures, symbols, or model forms.

The Inclusion Series
Resources for Educators, Paraprofessionals and Parents
from
Peytral Publications

Inclusion: 450 Strategies for Success by Peggy A. Hammeken
8 1/2" by 11" - 140 pages. $19.95 plus $3.00 shipping   ISBN -9644271-7-6

Since it's release in March of 1995, this book has received nationwide attention. It has been listed in numerous newsletters and magazines as an exceptional, practical, easy-to-use, and teacher friendly resource. This innovative book was selected as the *Editors' Choice* in the January-February 1996 issue of *Learning-Successful Teaching Today*. The article, *"Grappling with Inclusion Confusion"* was co-authored by Peggy Hammeken.

This valuable resource is written for general and special education teachers who teach students with special needs. Each inclusionary setting must be tailored to the school for which it is created. This book includes simple step-by-step guidelines to tailor your inclusionary setting. If you already have an existing setting, you will find many ideas to expand and improve the program. It also includes hundreds of practical teacher tested strategies which are numbered for quick easy reference. The strategies are listed by topics such as large group instruction, note taking skills, written language, math, spelling, attention difficulties, textbook modifications, and assessments to name a few. The book also includes many practical forms to help educators with all aspects of the inclusionary setting. This book is a valuable tool for general and special education teachers, teachers entering the field of education, Chapter I teachers and ESL teachers.

Inclusion: An Essential Guide for the Paraprofessional by Peggy A. Hammeken
8 1/2" by 11" - 140 pages $19.95 plus $3.00 shipping   ISBN - 9644271 - 6-8

In school districts across the nation, the number of paraprofessionals employed may be equal to or exceed the number of special education teachers, yet training for these vital members of the team is often overlooked. This is not intentional. Currently training has been focused on the general and special education teachers. Until educators are comfortable working within the new system, it is very difficult to provide training for the parapro-fessional. Therefore, the book, *Inclusion: An Essential Guide for the Paraprofessional* was written to meet this need. The new book may be used in conjunction with *Inclusion: 450 Strategies for Success* or it can stand alone.

The book includes everything the paraprofessional needs to know to work within the school system. This publication includes general information about inclusion, the due process system, handicapping conditions, labels, and the role of the multidisciplinary team members. Once the background has been established, the book covers meaningful topics such as, the paraprofessional's role, working collaboratively in the classroom environment, working with the general and special education teachers and students, communication tools, confidentiality, types of common teaching practices, levels of modifications, plus much more. The book also includes approximately 300 strategies for the paraprofessional to use when working with students. As with the first book, *Inclusion: 450 Strategies for Success*, valuable reproducible forms are included in the extensive, reproducible Appendix. These forms will assist the paraprofessional with communication, backup plans for medical and behavior emergencies, scheduling for substitutes and coordinating modification strategies, to name a few.

This book is an essential resource for paraprofessionals looking for a job, recently hired or for the experienced paraprofessional interested in refining their skills. This is also and excellent training and inservice tool for school districts to use with the training of paraprofessionals.

Living with ADHD: A Practical Guide to Coping with Attention Deficit Hyperactivity Disorder by Rebecca Kajander, CPNP, MPH.

7 1/4" by 10"   72 pages $9.95 plus $3.00 shipping   ISBN - 884153-08-9

This friendly, encouraging book is the perfect place to start for any parent who would like to learn more about ADHD. As with our previous publications, this book contains practical, easy-to-use tips that can help educators, parents and students cope with home, school and social settings. The book includes resources for parents and educators, if additional help and information is needed. The author is a pediatric nurse practitioner who has fifteen years of experience in the assessment and behavior management for students with ADHD.

The following quotes are taken from the back cover of this book. These quotes summarize the book.

"ADHD is a common developmental disorder that requires for its successful mastery well-developed coping skills 1) based on an understanding of its cause, manifestations and management, and 2) the informed joint participation of the child, the family and the school. This superb primer describes, in direct and detailed fashion, how this may be accomplished. It is the best such guide that I have had the pleasure of reviewing, and I highly recommend it to those who wish expert advice about rearing a child with ADHD." Morris Green, MD. Professor of Pediatrics - Indiana University School of Medicine- Riley Hospital for Children, Indianapolis.

"I am so impressed with this book. I found it reader friendly, not filled with medical and educational jargon. The ideas are concrete and practical. I can't wait to use some of them in my classroom and with parents at conference time. This book is a winner!" - Educator.

This practical easy to use book should be available to every parent who would like to learn more about ADHD. It is an excellent resource for all school districts to have in their reference libraries.

Peytral Publications

Discount Price List
School Districts and Universities
(Effective Jan. 1, 1995)

1 - 2	**No discount**
3 - 10	**10% discount**
11 - 20	**20% discount**
21 or more	**25% discount**

Terms: Our terms are net 30 days from the date of invoice. A finance charge of 1 1/2 % per month will be added to all overdue balances after 60 days.

Shipping: Books are shipped via the Post Office's book rate. Shipping/handling charge is $3.00 for the first book and $.50 for each additional book (rates subject to change without notice). We can also ship via UPS or Federal Express, rates vary. Shipping is FOB.

Shortages or non-receipt must be reported to us within 30 days of the order date.

Guarantee: Peytral Publications offers a satisfaction guarantee. If you are not satisfied return the books within 30 days, with a copy of the invoice and you will receive a 100% refund of your purchase price.

Orders may be sent to Peytral Publications, P.O. Box 1162B, Minnetonka, MN 55345. **Telephone** - (612) 949-8707 or **Fax** - (612) 906-9777.
PURCHASE ORDER OR CHECK MUST ACCOMPANY ALL ORDERS

ORDER FORM

Name:_____

Address:_____

City:_____ **State:**_____ **Zip:**_____

Quantity	Description	Unit price	Total
	Inclusion: 450 Strategies for Success	$19.95	
	Inclusion: An Essential Guide for the Paraprofessional	$19.95	
	Inclusion: A Practical Guide for Parents	$19.95	
	Inclusion books only - Less discount ___% (See chart above)		
	SUB TOTAL		
	Living with ADHD - A Practical Guide to Coping with Attention Deficit Hyperactivity Disorder **(Sorry, no discount available)**	$9.95	
	SHIPPING and HANDLING (See above)		
	TOTAL		

P.O. Box 1162, Minnetonka, MN 55345   Telephone (612) 949-8707 Fax (612) 906-9777